Praise for *Do Not Att*

"This is one of the most clear, engaging, I have ever read. I have written a few bo... more—and this truly is a great book. I was unable to stop reading it. Each chapter caused me to laugh or cry. Some of the authors' writing is so delicious that at the end of some of the chapters, I just wanted to have seconds. I have observed missions and missionaries, of course. What this book does so well is that it gives us not just an inside-out view of a mission, but of the missionary. We shortchange any missionary who enters her or his service without reading this book first."
  —Clayton Christensen, author of *Everyday Missionaries*

"Before my mission, I read everything I could read about what a mission would be like. There was nothing specifically for me, as a woman. Now there is. If you, or a woman you love, is thinking about a mission, run—but not in heels—to buy this book."
  —Whitney Johnson, popular *Harvard Business Review* blogger, author of *Dare, Dream, Do*

"The most frank and accurate description of mission life since the movie *The Best Two Years*. You'll find yourself crying on one page and laughing hysterically on the next. It's like EFY for missionaries! With the recent increase in the number of sister missionaries, this book is an absolute must read for any young woman who is thinking about serving."
  —Alonzo Gaskill, author of *The Truth about Eden*

"Hats off to Elise and Jennifer for compiling mission stories of faithful Latter-day Saint sisters. I cried, laughed, and was inspired by the adventures the sisters faced as they served the Lord Jesus Christ. Their obedience to the gospel and their willingness to stand up for the Church of Jesus Christ of Latter-day Saints gives me courage to do the same. The sisters' heartfelt expressions of faithfulness will long be remembered. *Do Not Attempt in Heels* is a must read for the missionary in each of us."
  —Susan Easton Black, bestselling author

foreword by CAMILLE FRONK OLSON

DO NOT ATTEMPT
in heels

{ MISSION STORIES *and* ADVICE
from SISTERS *who've* BEEN THERE }

compiled by

ELISE BABBEL HAHL &
JENNIFER ROCKWOOD KNIGHT

CFI
An Imprint of Cedar Fort, Inc.
Springville, Utah

ISBN 13: 978-1-4621-1391-0

Published by CFI, an imprint of Cedar Fort, Inc., 2373 W. 700 S., Springville, UT 84663
Distributed by Cedar Fort, Inc., www.cedarfort.com

LIBRARY OF CONGRESS CATALOGING-IN-PUBLICATION DATA

Do not attempt in heels : mission stories and advice from sisters who've been there / compiled by Elise Babbel Hahl and Jennifer Rockwood Knight; foreword by Camille Fronk Olson.
  pages cm
Includes bibliographical references.
ISBN 978-1-4621-1391-0
1. Mormon women missionaries. 2. Church of Jesus Christ of Latter-day Saints--Missions. I. Hahl, Elise, editor of compilation. II. Knight, Jennifer Rockwood, editor of compilation.

BX8661.D6 2014
266'.9332082--dc23

2013043257

Cover design by Shawnda T. Craig
Cover design © 2014 Lyle Mortimer
Edited and typeset by Emily S. Chambers

Printed in the United States of America

10 9 8 7 6 5 4 3 2 1

Printed on acid-free paper

Contents

CONTENTS

Foreword

Camille Frank Olson

n his opening address of general conference on October 6, 2012, President Thomas S. Monson publicized a new policy inviting young women to consider full-time missions sooner than ever before. "Today I am pleased to announce that able, worthy young women who have the desire to serve may be recommended for missionary service beginning at age nineteen, instead of age twenty-one." The explosive response from young women around the world wanting to serve has surpassed expectations and inspired Church members everywhere. That is what makes a book of essays like this one both timely and meaningful. Reading insightful, wise observations from experienced sister missionaries can be invaluable to young women trying to decide if and when to submit their papers and what to expect if they go.

It's a great gift to engage in the process of prayerfully considering whether to serve a mission. Although well-meaning and self-appointed advisors (such as friends, family members, or teachers) may disapprove of your decision, whether it is "yes" or "no," if you know your answer came from God, you can move forward with confidence. As one who applied that process and received the spiritual prompting to answer the call in my early twenties, I learned for the first time that my Father in Heaven really does have a plan for me. That realization has blessed me in making even more important decisions long after my full-time service.

Every one of these essays elicits tender and meaningful memories of my service decades ago. The details may differ, but the parallels with my mission are striking. Feelings of inadequacy, frustrations with inflexible companions, embarrassment over fashion faux pas, and poignant petitions for spiritual direction color young women's experiences in every land and era. I learned to appreciate Paul's admission that "I have planted, Apollos watered; but God gave the increase" (1 Corinthians 3:6) as I worked together with members to help investigators become contributing members of our faith community. If we are honest, however, we acknowledge that true conversion occurs only through the power of God. Being thus immersed in the Savior's work of salvation and redemption is humbling, and at the same time, confidence-producing. Like Paul, I came to know, "I can do all things through Christ which strengtheneth me" (Philippians 4:13).

An authentic voice permeates each essay, delineating lessons learned through trials, mistakes, and miracles. There are stories about poor health, long days, and homesickness—obstacles that can challenge even the most dedicated. Some of the authors had to learn to trust the Lord's timetable instead of their own and decipher greater blessings than numbers of baptisms—lessons that would bless them long after their missions.

Individually and collectively, these essays reinforce the truth that a mission forever changes the missionary and, as more than one discovered, "blessings of the mission never stop." For many of us, it was during our missions that we fell in love with the scriptures and overcame our fear of talking to strangers about our personal faith. A recurring miracle for imperfect missionaries is the way we learn to love those we teach, no matter how different they are from us, and how the missionary companion we think we can barely tolerate soon becomes a sister indeed. We rarely sign up for a mission to ride a bicycle in a skirt, tract in freezing cold temperatures, work and sleep in two days of sweat, watch doors slam in our faces, or follow an impression to travel a path, only to find it is covered with thorns. I remember the plastic poncho we wore while traveling by bike; the hood stayed in place when I turned my head and left the print of a "railroad track" around my face by the time I removed it. But I am genuinely thrilled when I hear one of my nieces or young women in my ward has a mission call because I know that a mission is far more than learning to do hard things. The confidence gleaned from knowing that God inspires, guides, and empowers His daughters during their missionary labors stays with them in fundamental ways when they return home.

In hindsight, I can trace my career path and post-graduate education to the fact that I was a returned missionary. Without question, my mission opened doors of unique opportunity for me. It also cemented in me the sure conviction that the gospel of Jesus Christ—as taught in the pages of the Bible and Book of Mormon and revealed to the Prophet Joseph Smith—is indeed true. I discovered my voice during my mission and believe God then provided me opportunities to articulate and demonstrate how Christ and His gospel informs, enriches, and empowers men and women everywhere.

With this growing army of confident, committed, and grounded sister missionaries, there is great hope for the future—for strong marriages, families, and communities at a time when greed and selfishness too often erode them. So stand back and cheer as young women throughout the Church set aside high heels in order to march out and serve.

Introduction

You're thinking seriously about a mission and wondering what it would really be like to serve one. You've gone on splits with the missionaries and read letters from friends or older sisters who decided to go. Maybe you've watched *Errand of Angels* and imagined what it would be like to serve a mission with such a fabulous collection of scarves. Or you've gone out to dinner with a returned elder who gave lots of advice about his mission, some of which will apply to your mission, some of which won't. (And based on personal experience, if, out of all the advice he could possibly offer, he shares the sensitive little gem, "Don't come home unless it's in a box," you should order the most expensive thing on the menu. Seriously!) Even after all this information-gathering, and even if you've prepared for a mission your entire life, you're still in for a few surprises.

We can't tell you the exact surprises you'll face, because each mission and missionary is unique. (One of our writers learned she had a sloth living in her backyard in her first area.) Still, we want to help you manage whatever comes your way. We're hoping our stories can be like the good senior companion who puts her arm around you at the end of a hard day and makes you laugh. We've trudged through the longest days of our life on our missions, survived rodent problems, fought off homesickness, and fallen asleep on our knees. We've also forged eternal friendships, experienced the miracle of finding someone ready to listen, and felt close to heaven as we watched people we love walk into the baptismal font.

As any good senior companion would, we're going to share our secrets about the times we did things right—the times that made us proud. We want you to have lots of these moments on your mission. And we want to reassure you that when you walk off the plane at the end of your mission, you'll be much stronger than the day you walked wide-eyed into the MTC, a heavy suitcase in tow.

Every one of the writers in this collection was a rock-star missionary, the kind that any mission president would want on his team. We even found some of these writers through the recommendations of mission presidents themselves. Even so, you'll notice a lot of struggling in these essays. If we can offer a word of advice right here in the introduction, it would be this: Don't be afraid of struggling on your mission; it's going to happen. It's through the hard times that you emerge wiser, more Christlike, and better equipped to understand your own investigators, who are struggling to change too. As missionaries, we have to spend "at least a few moments in Gethsemane," as Elder Holland said, in order to understand better what Christ did for us.[1]

Even though you won't see many books about women serving missions on bookstore shelves, as a sister missionary, you'll be joining a proud tradition. The very first missionaries to preach the Resurrection of Christ were sisters, in fact. Mary Magdalene, Joanna, Salome, and the mother of James discovered the empty tomb before anyone else. An angel proclaimed, "He is risen; he is not here. . . . But go your way, tell his disciples and Peter that he goeth before you" (Mark 16:6–7). After receiving this

---

1 Jeffrey R. Holland, "Missionary Work and the Atonement," *Ensign* March, 2011.

special charge, these women ran—yes they ran—to tell the eleven remaining Apostles what they had witnessed. According to Luke, the apostles didn't believe the women at first because they thought they were telling "idle tales" (Luke 24:11). Once Peter and John checked the tomb themselves, they realized that the sisters were right: Christ had truly risen. And the sisters were the first missionaries called to proclaim His Resurrection.

Should you choose to serve, you'll be walking, pedaling, and running all over the place to preach Christ's gospel too. You may preach the gospel on a tundra in Siberia or a sidewalk in New Jersey. You may knock on doors in Paris, France, or Paris, Missouri. But wherever you may serve, take this one last piece of advice about missions to heart: Do not attempt in heels! (We're not kidding.) In the end, the most attractive footwear is the kind that allows you to work all day. The scriptures say it best: "How beautiful upon the mountains are the feet of [her] that bringeth good tidings, that publisheth peace; that bringeth good tidings of good, that publisheth salvation; that saith unto Zion, Thy God reigneth!" (Isaiah 52:7).

That's true in every mission.

Pioneers in Plastic Boots

Jessie Hawkes

I spent the first three weeks in Nebraska jogging in two feet of slushy snow behind Sister Worthen, watching the Day-Glo orange snow shovel bounce on her shoulder. The heavy rubber boots I purchased on my first P-day in Nebraska slipped loosely around my calves. Initially, I had donned my fashionable, heeled, and completely insufficient leather boots over three pairs of SmartWool socks, but after a week of losing feeling in my toes, I succumbed to this frumpier pair.

There we were, running through the neighborhood, Sister Worthen charging ahead of me in her ankle-length coat, looking distinctly like a puffy, black weasel. I shuffled my way up the snow-packed walkway with a backpack, new boots, and a restrictive knee-length coat. Ugh.

Suddenly, Sister Worthen screeched to a halt ahead of me and I almost knocked her over on the ice. At five foot four, I wasn't tall, but I stood a good four inches above my tiny firecracker of a companion. She looked up at me with large blue eyes and impossibly long lashes.

"Sister! Do you remember Brother Kesler? He's the bald guy you met on Sunday." I nodded vigorously and panted in the steamy air, while mentally sorting through all the men in the ward experiencing various degrees of baldness. No recollections. Sister Worthen steamed ahead. "Great. Okay, well, his mother-in-law lives here—well, she used to be his mother-in-law, but then she got divorced, remember? From the old guy with the four dogs? And moved up here. His old house was in the green area, I pointed it out to you on Tuesday." I gave up on the façade of recollection and just rearranged my face into what I hoped to be a bewildered, yet sensitive look.

"Uh . . ."

"Great. We'll shovel her walk."

I felt my heart slip a few degrees south. We had been shoveling driveways for almost a week now, and my arms and back were tired from slinging the thick Nebraska snow. I fumbled with the elastic sleeve of my heavy coat, peeling it back with my glove to reveal my watch.

"Well, wait, don't we have a lesson with the Spillmans at 5:30? I bet if we left now we would be just a few minutes early . . ." But before the sentence had even found its finish, Sister Worthen had thrown herself furiously into the task. Snow flew into mounds on both sides as she set to work with characteristic intensity. I sighed, slid my backpack onto the icy sidewalk, and started in with my own blue shovel.

Scrape, pull, toss. Scrape, pull, toss. I did the math one more time: it would require three weeks of eating only ramen and orange juice to purchase a snowblower from Walmart on our missionary stipend. Rats. *Scrape, pull, toss.* Ahead, Sister Worthen bustled up the drive (*rattle fling! rattle fling!*), the snow flying in a continuous cascade over her shoulder. How did she do it? *Scrape, pull, toss.* It wasn't that I was unhappy. Ever since I was a little girl, I had wanted to serve a mission. Like many sisters I knew, though, the decision had been a challenge for me because I was afraid of "making the wrong choice." *Scrape, pull, toss.* I had been halfway finished with my mission application—*scrape*—when I was

6

attacked with—*pull*—sudden doubts about—*toss*—missing an opportunity to date a boy I loved and fears that my missionary service was a subconscious escape from graduation. *Scrape.* Feeling that God was not answering my prayers, I floundered in indecision until my mother finally prodded me to cancel my tuition, sell my contract, and stay home until the call came. *Pull.* Spiritual confirmation came shortly afterward, and I had felt calm and excited about my decision ever since. *Toss.* Another shovel-worth of snow flopped onto the lawn. The sky and the snow were a uniform off-gray canvas, punctuated by the dark, wet arms of trees. I was feeling warmer, grateful for the exercise, although my abs began to twinge with exertion after a month of underuse in the MTC. No, I was happy to be a missionary. I flipped another mound of snow onto the walk, grating the metal rim of the shovel against the asphalt. I just hadn't expected to be so, well, tired.

When I really look at it, feeling tired and cold in Winter Quarters shouldn't have been much of a surprise to me. I mean, I was assigned to spend a huge part of my mission in the Mormon Trail Center at Historic Winter Quarters, where my job was to depict the struggle of nature and faith to our guests. Their stories were particularly poignant to me because we walked the same streets and endured the same storms.

In 1846, Nebraska was a proving ground for the early members of the Church of Jesus Christ of Latter-day Saints. As temperatures fell below freezing, Saints huddled in their sod huts and tiny log cabins, fending off the cold and rampantly spreading disease. Tuberculosis, malaria, scurvy, and chills claimed almost 400 lives. The pioneers, already exhausted from a muddy slog across 365 miles of Iowa were grateful to have a place to stay but discouraged at yet another diversion on the road to Zion. With faith, they hurried to erect 800 cabins and sod huts, in desperation even digging

.

cave-like lean-tos into the side of the Nebraska hills. Some of the less fortunate or late arrivals camped under the canvas of their wagons for the duration of the winter.

When the snow was too brittle with cold to be pried up from the asphalt driveways of Omaha, I thought of the pioneers in wool coats and soggy leather boots, attempting to saw down trees and chink the sides with frozen mud. My own physical sacrifices were pathetic at best. On cold days, I was forced to stop wearing mascara because my warm breath would steep through my scarf and freeze on my eyelids, causing any makeup to run rivers down my cheeks. I missed my attractive thin leather boots every time I put on my hearty plastic and faux-fur lined stompers, a thirteen dollar sale from the Bellevue Walmart. We were on foot on the days with the heaviest snow, as maneuvering our Toyota Corolla through the thick Nebraska weather was deemed too risky. Small as these sacrifices were, it only seemed right that we would continue the pioneers' tradition of suffering in Nebraska's stormy winters and unforgiving wind. In the gray winter months, I was just grateful that I could bear up my yoke with an 800-fill down coat and a three-month supply of "Lil' Hotties" hand warmers.

One night, after a cloudy evening of knocking on doors that stayed closed (disappointing) and a few doors that actually opened (terrifying), Sister Worthen and I returned to our car for our final hour and a half of teaching before we could retreat to our home. Lowering myself into the seat of our small car, I felt my mission zest wilt. It was cold. I was afraid of talking to people and equally weary from rushing door to door. I slumped in the seat next to my fearless companion, recognizing the wash of self-pity but feeling helpless to rise from it.

Sister Worthen glanced over at me as she started the car and coughed quietly. "Ah, want to hear a story? It's from a pioneer named Francis Webster." She adjusted the heating vents and then turned her clear eyes straight to me, gleaming with the power that brought children, animals, and investigators directly to her side. She quoted:

"'I have pulled my hand cart when I was so weak and weary from illness and lack of food that I could hardly put one foot ahead of the other. I have looked ahead and seen a patch of sand or a hill slope and I have said I can go only that far and there I must give up for I cannot pull the load through it. I have gone on to that sand and when I reached it the cart began pushing me. I have looked back many times to see who was pushing my cart but my eyes saw no one. I knew then that the angels of God were there.

"'Was I sorry that I chose to come by hand cart? No. Neither then nor any minute of my life since. The price we paid to become acquainted with God was a privilege to pay and I am thankful that I was privileged to come in the Martin Handcart Company.'" [2]

She beamed at me for a moment. "Sister, you are doing great. You can do this." Then she released the emergency brake and we zipped off to the next appointment.

That story warmed my memory for the duration of that first difficult winter. The more porches I stood on and dogs I petted and driveways I shoveled, the more I realized just how much God loves His children. Like, really loves them. I would have a three-minute conversation with a sixteen-year-old boy on his driveway and find myself praying for him that night. I saw God responding to our investigators' prayers by bringing good friends to their home, providing a working car in a time of need, restoring a long-lost conviction of purpose, and bringing food when there was little hope.

---

2 "Pioneer Women," *Relief Society Magazine*, Jan. 1948, 8.

As I saw Heavenly Father's loving responses to His children, I also began to recognize the moments when I felt God pushing my little handcart up the proverbial mountain of missionary work. Like Francis Webster, I came to know Him more personally. This was a time on my mission when I had been invited to pray for thirty minutes each night; each evening found me crouched over my planner and sticky notes by the night-light, pleading for a softer heart, a desire to teach His children, miracles for our investigators, and a conviction of truth for myself. Suddenly, I didn't care so much about feeling tired. I felt grace turn my heart away from the challenges of the work and toward the needs of our investigators. In our tiny study room in Bellevue, Nebraska, I felt the Lord fulfill His promise to me: "Or what man is there of you, whom if his son ask bread, will he give him a stone? Or if he ask a fish, will he give him a serpent? If ye then, being evil, know how to give good gifts unto your children, how much more shall your Father which is in heaven give good things to them that ask him?" (Matthew 7:9–11).

That winter, I really spoke to God for the first time in my twenty-one years and He shaped and chastened my rough, childish heart. Like the Savior taught, I saw God deliver bread instead of stones to my hungry hands.

Recognizing God working in my life carried me out of my first area and into my second, which proved to be flatter and more remote, with more fields and rural mansions. I arrived in the middle of July, when the air was a hot, damp breath until the weekly thunderstorm boiled in. Due to some disobedient missionaries in the past, the ward had a bad taste in their mouth when it came to missionary work, so we spent our time trying to rebuild relationships and talk to as many people as would step outside their homes in the heat. Slowly, the doors of members and investigators alike began opening. For the rest of the summer and fall, I stayed in the area. By the time winter rolled around, I had outlasted three different companions until I knew every street in the area and every name on the ward list.

I spent a total of nine months in that area roaming within the same twenty-mile radius, in a stretch of time that felt like my own personal journey to Zion. Here I was brought to my knees with the responsibility of two companions fresh from the MTC, and I pled to know how to help them, to find investigators to build their faith, to drive the tangled Omaha highway system without getting lost. Revelation became tangible and real as we received hourly promptings about who to visit. It was so different from my vaguely fuzzy experiences with the Spirit in my earlier life. Instead we had stumbled through the static to a clear connection with the Spirit, and we felt the Lord's voice with clarity and sharpness: love, correction, guidance, encouragement, forgiveness, mercy. One of my companions and I realized mid-transfer that we hadn't listened to music in weeks, we were too caught up in discussion to bother with it. We had almost no one to teach, but we were blissfully happy. We were wandering in the wilderness of the Midwest, sure that we would see some pillar of fire just behind the next condominium, murmuring glory as it evaporated into the prairie sky.

Zion was in our hearts long before we saw a baptism. It must have been the same with the Saints; the feeling of refuge began miles before the Salt Lake mountains puckered the horizon. Of this journey, Brigham Young said,

> You that have not passed through the trials, and persecu
> tions ... but have only read of them ... may think how awful they
> were to endure, and wonder that the Saints survived them at all.
> The thought of it makes your hearts sink within you . . . and

you are ready to exclaim, "I could not have endured it." I have been in the heat of it, and I never felt better in all my life; I never felt the peace and power of the Almighty more copiously poured upon me than in the keenest part of our trials.[3]

Brother Brigham speaks here of a real power of overcoming, the power of the Atonement of Jesus Christ that comes into our lives through an immersion of the Spirit. I know that he is speaking of the pioneers, but in my mind, his conviction brings to mind mornings kneeling on the shabby beige carpet and laughing with my companion on the wraparound porches of Midwestern manors, swept in the generous gold of a Nebraska sun.

Thirteen months after my snowy transfer hobbling after Sister Worthen, I cried with excitement at the baptisms of Lauren and Ashley. Watching the beautiful mom and her radiant eleven-year-old daughter, I recalled the months of prayers and fasting my companions and I had undergone to see them to this point. I sat next to Lauren, her brown hair bobbing slightly as she sang along with the words of the hymn, "I am a Child of God." I felt like a proud parent and wrapped my arm around her, squeezing her thin shoulders into my side.

I remembered how timid both Ashley and her mother had been when we had first appeared on their doorstep on a late December evening. And here they were, coffee-free, wearing white, and certain of God's love. Their journey had been a daily struggle against family pressure and fear and discouragement. While proud and excited for their actual baptism, I knew that today was only a step in their continued conversion. Their baptism represented a covenant with God and indicated previous months of personal experiences with Him.

Sitting in the Primary room with my arm around Lauren, I

3 *Deseret News Weekly*, 24 August 1854, 83.

realized that I could say the same thing about my mission. While baptisms were wonderful and rewarding, some of the most powerful experiences came as my companion and I talked about the progress of investigators on the drive home to our apartment, or during a particularly faith-promoting street contact or lesson with a new investigator. The "big" days—baptisms and zone conferences—were merely milestones plotted onto the much vaster landscape of my mission experience. It was through the daily and hourly associations with God and His children that my mission became the complex and personal experience that I remember now. I look over this time of my life with complicated feelings: deep joy and gratitude intermixed with sharp regret for episodes of impatience with investigators and prideful moments with my companions.

Mapped throughout all of it, though, is the Atonement of Jesus Christ; not just the forgiving part but the enabling part— the part that miraculously made me eager to throw on my coat and rush out the door with my poor junior companion in tow. It made me better than I could have been on my own. I learned to love better, listen more, aim higher. I saw the Lord's hand not only in my own changes, but in the little things happening in the world around me. Gorgeous prairie clouds, a letter from a friend, a powerful first lesson, a note of encouragement from a companion, a new investigator at church; in Nebraska these were the placeholders of grace. Now I see this power in texts from my mother, in the energy to comfort a friend or teach a class, in the courage to leave an old habit and begin anew daily, in the promptings to step out into a life open and uncertain—all reminders of a loving God who knows all His children, whose name is Endless, whose arms reach through the confusion of clammy days and sleepless nights to touch us.

JESSIE HAWKES graduated from Brigham Young University in English in 2013. She spent her last semester studying the conversion stories of Polynesian pioneer women in Hawaii. She loves running, writing, backpacking, and rock climbing. She published scholarly work on Emily Dickinson while at BYU, as well as several personal essays on charitable giving, idealism, and the relationship between the spirit and the body.

Becoming a Leading Lady

Sharon Belnap Seminario

The wooden floor creaked and crackled as each of us knelt down clumsily in our dresses and skirts for our first bedtime hymn and prayer in Nauvoo. Well, I knelt down clumsily. The tall, blonde sister with sky blue eyes next to me was the picture of grace, surely immune to such inadequacies. Across from me, a Shirley Temple look-alike sat cozily in the circle, smiling from ear to ear. She played three instruments and clogged, so I was sure anything this mission threw at her would be cotton candy. I looked around at these strangers, people who would spend every day with me leading tours throughout Old Nauvoo and bearing testimony through song, acting, and dance. The auburn-haired sister with classic film beauty suggested a hymn. I could instantly sense her musical confidence and strong sense of self. I guessed that she was the sister with one music degree under her belt and another degree about to begin at a far-away, prestigious college. I was sure she was qualified to give singing lessons to somebody like me. Another sister gave the starting note. I would come to find out that she had perfect pitch and heard music constantly in the sounds of life: the microwave beep (B flat!), the whirring of a car motor (A natural!), the buzzing of a bee (C sharp!). At least I had a ballpark idea of where those notes *were* on a piano.

We eight brand-new sisters were finishing our first day as performing missionaries in Nauvoo by gathering in our new

quarters, the David Yearsley home (where the Young Men's orga-
nization has its origins). Once we began to sing the hymn, I
could tell I was out of my league. Way out. An operatic vibrato
floated above the air, coming somewhere from this mix of sisters.
I would have paid good money to listen to a voice like that in a
concert! An alto voice, probably peeled straight from Broadway,
rose forcefully against the melody. I knew some of those sisters had played every role known to womankind in professional
musical theater, from *West Side Story*'s Maria to Maria Von Trapp.
My one lead role as a crazy nun in our high school musical
wasn't exactly ingénue level, and I preferred to sing in a choir
setting where I could blend in.

In retrospect, my recording of our hymn that first night sounds
a little to me like eight soloists outdoing each other. We were singing in harmony, but we didn't sing "in harmony." Not yet. We just
weren't "one." And on top of that, I felt like the weakest link. I
loved to sing, but I was very, very blessed to be among such tal-
ented and accomplished musicians.

The next morning, our Visitor's Center Director (and future
mission president), Elder Sager, asked me to serve as the "house
manager." My knees went numb and wobbly. I felt surprised and
honored by the opportunity, but more than a little unsure. Having
already labeled myself as one of the more meager talents in the
group, I was not expecting a leadership role of any kind. I was
younger than many of the sisters, didn't have any experience
living on my own or with roommates, and only a week before had
depended on my mother for clean socks. But for whatever reason
I was asked. I was going to be expected to see to the order of the
home and the cohesion of the sisters therein, address disputes with
tact, and more or less problem-solve to achieve as many positive
results as possible.

I have so many journal entries lamenting my abilities as house manager. I encountered challenges completely new to me. Group cohesion was the first thing to think about. Although every single sister was wonderful and was dedicated to giving her all, we had glaring differences. One sister had only brothers, one had only sisters (so they were companions, of course). One was the youngest in her family, a couple of sisters were the oldest in their families; one sister had lived away from home for years, and others were homesick living away from home for the first time. We had sisters who came with special health needs and a sister who developed a serious health problem during our service. The main thing aside from the gospel that we all had in common was our involvement in music and theater. So the stage was set for infusing the ordinary with an extra measure of drama.

The other main challenges to my job as house manager were smaller, furrier, big-eared, and long-tailed. The David Yearsley home sat next to a huge, open field. So naturally, we were in a full-on raging war with mice from the minute we set foot in the place.

Because we had a rodent problem, our rules for cleanliness in the Yearsley home had to be strict and precisely followed. We had mice trying to live in our clothing, eat our food, and surprise us in the restroom. That's not the kind of surprise most sisters enjoyed.

As house manager I tried a few tactics to combat the mice. I bought a sound machine that was supposed to put out a frequency to drive the mice far from the house. Instead, I think the mice had a nightly dance party to the sound. We tried to keep crumbs swept, our garbage tied up, and our laundry un-smellable. A very unsettled sister started ranting about a mouse sighting one night. I was fed up with the little invaders. I dressed up as a mice-fighting superhero, sporting a spontaneous costume of headache-gel mask, flyswatter, gloves, and a scarf, and tried to intimidate the critters as I ran around up and down the stairs and in and out of rooms. I really showed them who was boss.

We had to be vigilant about cleanliness, particularly with food, in order to avoid disease and a constant gross-out factor. We had spaces allotted for each companionship's goods in the kitchen cupboards, and everyone was supposed to keep her food well contained in either that space or our one small fridge. (There really was only one fridge for eight sisters. And we only got to shop once a week. On the same day. Not exactly a pioneer hardship, but nearly.)

My companion and I had the only lower cupboard space, so we knew that hoards of the lazier mice would try to snack on our Mini-Wheats. One mouse kept breaking into our cracker box, so we finally taped it shut at night to be safe. In the morning we woke up and went to our cupboard, eager to gloat and glory in our victory. What did we find? A personal message from the little guy! He left his droppings squarely on top of our securely taped box. It's hard to say who won that battle.

These fractious conditions set the stage for one of the most difficult experiences I had as house manager. Because of busy mission work and P-days spent seeing the historic sights, we had reached a point where the house was more than untidy. All of us had food out of place in the kitchen. The whole house was turning into a clutter swamp and there could be no more. On the morning of the following preparation day I announced we'd have a group clean-up.

I ran around to every room and requested with the subtlety of an alarm clock that everyone needed to come—now—to the kitchen and clean. After a few minutes, most everyone had gathered and sisters began straightening and wiping and eliminating. Progress! I was washing dishes vigorously when to my dismay, I suddenly noticed that one of the sisters was not cleaning. She was sitting, *sitting*, in the living room. Didn't she hear me say it was time to clean? Didn't she know that we were waiting on her to remove her stuff from the cupboard counter?! How could she sit calmly in the eye of this disinfecting whirlwind and do nothing?! I took a deep breath.

"Sister Miles," I sweetly called. "We're having a group clean-up, just letting you know." I felt it my duty to gently correct her. After all it was my responsibility to lead, especially in situations like this!

Pause.

"Okay, thanks for letting me know," she said with a dismissive lilt, not making eye contact. I tried not to react. I washed more dishes. I watched peripherally as sisters came and went with clutter from their rooms, organized their cupboards, and pulled moldy cauliflower from the fridge drawer.

"I think we'll be done soon," I called out again, indirectly, but aiming every word at Sister Miles. If I called out sweetly the first time, this time I called out with candy-coated poison darts. No response. I glanced over and saw Sister Miles carefully writing in her *journal*! What made her feel superior enough that she could watch us all clean around her while she did what she pleased?! I began to feel the blood coursing through my veins.

I walked directly over to the living room, my hands dripping with the hard work I had been doing for the last hour. *Without* her help. *Without* her respect.

"Sister Miles." I masked an even tone. "We are all cleaning and it is very important that we keep the house rules and that we all work together on this, so could you come and help us clean for a while?" I stood back, proud of my restraint, considering her insurrection.

Sister Miles put down her pen. She put down her notebook. She looked me squarely in the eyes and with concerted effort to press the tears down and keep them from choking her message said, "Sister Belnap. I was having one of the most spiritual experiences I have had in my life. I was trying to record that and really understand and ponder the feelings and impressions I received. And now, because of *you*, I can't!" And she thundered in a blur out of the room.

I stood there with my mouth and eyes wide as craters. If I had been slapped I would not have felt more stung. Every word she said burned into me like a cattle brand. I walked back to the sink, stuck my soapy hands back in the water, mindlessly scrubbed, and cried.

For a minute I crafted as many reasons as possible as to why I was innocent and she was in the wrong. But after a minute I gave up. Her words didn't sting because they were mean. I didn't cry because I was wronged. I felt sad and ashamed because I recognized I hadn't been the leader I should have been.

I could have given the sisters more notice. I could have put myself in her place and imagined that she must have a good reason for her actions. I could have asked her, "How's it going? What are you up to?" rather than informing her over and over again like a nagging goat that she was not doing what I wanted her to do when I wanted her to do it. I could have chilled out! I realized at that moment that I was doing a lot more pushing than leading.

It was true that in that setting I was supposed to be the leader, but maybe I was thinking of leading in the wrong way. I was too focused on results instead of method, on house instead of humans. I apologized later and Sister Miles very generously let it go. I made a goal to jump to conclusions less and to try to be more focused on spiritual things. I realized that as a leader I had been choosing what I saw as the needs of the many over the needs of the one. I wanted to lead like the Savior would lead, and I knew that He was an advocate of just the opposite. From that point on, I was a different sort of leader.

Instead of harping on everyone to do chores, when I saw something that needed to be done, I just did it. I humbled myself and thought more about serving than leading, as in Doctrine and Covenants 50:26, "He that is ordained of God and sent forth, the same is appointed to be the greatest, notwithstanding he is the least and the servant of all."

We always entered the house through the kitchen, and our shoes left prints and film and guck. So I woke up extra early several mornings and tiptoed like a stealthy mantis down the creaky wooden stairs so I wouldn't rouse any passed-out pioneer sisters. The sunshine flooded past the glaring gap at the top of the hill above our home where a temple once stood (and would stand again soon), glistened through our tiny paned window, and spread over our trafficked linoleum floor. The effect of the light illuminated all of the floor's flaws. At least I knew where to scrub.

I put on my headphones and pressed play. The comforting voices and hymns of the most recent general conference filled my ears and mind. I got down on my hands and knees in my T-shirt and my bloomers from my period costume. With a rag in my hand, I polished that old, worn floor from corner to corner with hot, soapy water.

The linoleum squares went from muddy to hazy to white during Elder Maxwell's "Hope Through the Atonement of Jesus Christ."[4] Somehow, the physical labor I did as I listened helped me to concentrate on the words, and they lingered in my mind long

---

4 Neal A. Maxwell, "Hope Through the Atonement of Christ," *Ensign*, November, 1998.

after the duration of the chore itself. Elder Maxwell gave the talk while bald from cancer treatments: instant context to every word he spoke. He taught me that often "we who wear wristwatches seek to counsel Him who oversees cosmic clocks and calendars."[5]

As I moved the rag across the floor, he testified to me, teaching me about my role as house manager with applications that stretched much further in my life. "Because God wants us to come home after having become more like Him and His Son, part of this developmental process, of necessity, consists of showing unto us our weaknesses. Hence, if we have ultimate hope we will be submissive, because, with His help, those weaknesses can even become strengths."[6]

As I followed the Spirit down a new path of leadership, I began to feel my weaknesses fade and to see strengths develop. New ideas came springing out of the better relationships I had with my sisters. I had a thought one day to have Christmas in July. The words no sooner left my lips than everybody jumped on the idea. Together we infused the holiday with excitement and merriment—stockings and carols and expressions of love. It was a wonderful, unifying day that made a lasting memory. In general, I stopped over-worrying about the house and the rules and made the most of our time. At the end of many hot and hurried days, we sat out on our porch looking over fields (filled with sleeping mice), wrote poems, sang songs, giggled, and watched fireflies waltz through the air and fade into the stars.

I also decided to listen more. Every day an opportunity would arise to walk or sit or cook or study with one of the eight sisters. I was able to laugh and think with them—to learn more about the life and struggles of each one. It gave me the chance to know

5 Ibid.
6 Ibid.

these amazing daughters of God in a deeper way. I learned so much from the wisdom with which they handled their problems and in return, I received advice from them on how to face my own challenges. I felt how important it was to each one to please her Father in Heaven and to do His will no matter what. I had the opportunity to sincerely compliment them on the spiritual gifts I saw in them that blessed my life, the lives of the other missionaries and even the visitors to Nauvoo. I look back in time and these moments of one-on-one listening and sharing are treasures in my memory: crystallized and glittering and sacred.

I came to feel that each sister could truly say I was her friend, at least. In retrospect, those relationships became so much more important to me than any great act as a leader. Instead of saying "lead one another," Jesus said, "Love one another, as I have loved you. Greater love hath no man than this, that a man lay down his life for his friends. Ye are my friends, if ye do whatsoever I command you" (John 15:12–14). Any degree of effectiveness I had as a leader, as house manager in Nauvoo, was directly proportional to the love I had for my friends and the ability I had to let my love for them eclipse myself and my will.

By the time we tearfully sang "Farewell, Nauvoo" before flying home, our sound had changed so much from that first night. Some of our more timid singers now sang with confidence. Many of us had learned to improvise new alto or descant lines with each other during our many hours of service together. Our opera-singing sister could easily meld her vibrato with the other voices so that it was unrecognizable, adding richness to the texture of the whole. We weren't thinking about words or tone or pitch. We felt the music. We were in tune. There were no soloists, but there was one voice. We sang in harmony in every way, and it was as natural as the steady flow of the wide Mississippi River.

After serving in Nauvoo, SHARON BELNAP SEMINARIO graduated in English-creative writing at BYU and with an MA in American studies-folklore at Utah State University. She loves to travel with her husband, Fernando; home schools her four children Miranda, Samuel, Mateo, and Victor; and teaches English composition at local colleges. This year she's a new member of the Mormon Tabernacle Choir and is expecting child number five.

Sweet Lemons

Mary Jones Scoresby

My hands trembled as I tore into the oversized white envelope containing my mission call. I saw my own eager anticipation reflected in the faces of dear family and friends who had gathered to share this milestone. In an instant, all the nervous chitchat, banter, and predictions that had filled the room were replaced with my voice alone. "Dear Sister Jones: You are hereby called to serve as a missionary of The Church of Jesus Christ of Latter-day Saints. You are assigned to labor in the Italy Rome Mission."

As soon as I read the word "Italy," the rest of the words on the page began to blur, dissolving into images of picturesque cobblestone streets lined with red geraniums and rolling green hills spotted with quaint villas. My mind raced forward to fill in the details of the next eighteen months of my life. My companion and I, dressed in chic black with only a name tag to distinguish us from the fashionable natives, would stroll past the Spanish steps or the Trevi fountain accompanied by the strains of Puccini and Verdi's most beloved arias. The pure in heart throughout Rome would flock to us, eager to hear the fulness of the gospel declared to them in impeccable Italian from two fresh-faced Americans. Our discussions would be a seamless sequence of truth, testimony, and tears. At the end of a long, yet fulfilling day of teaching appointments, the scent of garlic, basil, garden tomatoes, Parmesan cheese, and homemade pasta would welcome us home. And for dessert? Gelato, of course! I knew in that instant that Rome was the perfect mission for me.

The excited shrieks of family and friends soon shook me from my reverie. Italy. I was going to Italy! I first fell in love with all things Italian during an art history class in high school. The Italian masters Michelangelo, Caravaggio, and Bernini inspired me to declare myself as a humanities major at BYU without even a semester's deliberation. The art, music, literature, and architecture of Italy occupied a majority of my studies. All humanities majors were required to select a foreign language to specialize in and, serendipitously, I had chosen Italian and already had three semesters under my belt. I had also enjoyed the rigorous religion courses offered and scored an A in Mission Prep. In short, I was made for this mission. Italy and I would be a perfect combination.

On a cold but clear January morning, I arrived at the MTC with a heart as full as my two meticulously packed suitcases. Everything in my life had prepared me for this moment, it seemed. Blessings appeared instantly in the form of a dedicated companion and three inspiring teachers. I threw myself into the experience, always striving to meet the high expectations of family, leaders, teachers, and—most of all—myself. More than anything, I wanted a mission of no regrets. I was confident that if I could do everything exactly right, I would be a successful missionary. I left the MTC with a head full of memorized discussions and scriptures, and a heart eager to love and serve the Italian people. My wonderful teachers there had lit a fire under the departing districts. We would be the ones to change the landscape of the church in Italy, they promised. We would fill the fonts and chapels with families ready to accept the gospel. We would see a temple built in the very city that Paul visited as a missionary centuries ago.

Fast forward several months and I found myself in circumstances dramatically different from the naïve vision that accompanied my mission call. Dealing with insomnia, difficult companions, lack of investigators, and failing branches had drained me. Just four months after my MTC high, I wrote in my journal:

> This morning I woke up completely empty. I felt dry, like I had absolutely nothing left to give. I had zero energy, zero motivation, and zero desire. During my mission, I've felt sick, tired, frustrated, but I don't think I've ever felt such complete apathy. I know that these feelings don't come from God. I know that the Lord is counting on me to do His work here, but I don't know if I have it in me. My dad told me that there is nothing I could be doing as important as what I'm doing now. Then why do I want to be anywhere else?

How did this happen? I was discouraged and confused. I had followed the perfect formula with care and precision. Preparation, study, prayer, and obedience were supposed to equal success. My daily reality, however, looked nothing like the picture-perfect mission I had envisioned before I came. Instead of rushing from appointment to appointment or planning baptismal services, my companions and I typically spent several hours each day ringing doorbells in an apartment complex or trying to stop people on the street. We rarely found anyone who would listen to the first discussion, and those we did find almost never accepted an invitation for a return appointment. I remember the thrill of finishing a second discussion with a family, only to discover that even after learning about Joseph Smith, the Restoration, and the Book of Mormon, they were surprised to discover that we were not representatives from the Catholic Church and invited us to leave. Discouragement became my persistent shadow. I woke up each morning feeling defeated and lay awake at night counting my disappointments.

Overcoming the discouragement took place slowly and in stages. I can't point to just one conversation, one hymn, one prayer, one scripture or conference talk that fixed my broken dreams of a perfect mission, although all of them played a role. Rather, each time I cracked open the door of my heart to the influence of the Spirit, I felt nudged closer and closer to a "perfect brightness of hope" (2 Nephi 31:20). I started to understand more about agency. Prior to my mission, I thought about obedience in terms of a vending machine. That is, I believed that I could drop in coins of obedience and God would pop out blessings into my waiting hand. I realized on my mission that while I could be perfectly obedient to every mission rule, study diligently, and pray fervently, our investigators could still choose to reject the gospel. My coins of perfect obedience could not buy me the reward of baptisms. I could not control others' choices. I learned that when I submitted my own agency to Heavenly Father's will (such as, those things within my control like my time, attitude, habits, and desires), I was blessed—not with converts, but with the Spirit. The Spirit lightened my load; missionary work no longer felt like a burden.

Before these realizations, I had painfully watched my dream of a perfect mission crumble because I had stopped believing. I no longer believed my companion and I could find a family to teach. I no longer believed that our tiny branch would grow out of that old, rented apartment and into a ward. I no longer believed I would see a temple built in Rome. All of the promises my MTC teachers had made felt hollow. Trapped in the narrow confines of my own eighteen-month mission, I was right. Not one of those promises came true, at least not in the way I thought they would. To construct a new dream of a mission perfect in Christ, I needed to lean heavily on the Spirit to have faith in blessings I couldn't see.

Vincenzo Guariglia was the perfect blessing. "Enzo" was a widower and a true Italian gentleman. My companion and I would pass him most mornings in one of the main piazzas of Salerno, close to our bus stop. He would tip his wool cap to us, comment on the weather, and observe whether or not we had dressed accordingly. Intrigued by two young foreigners so far from home, he showed grandfatherly concern for us. He repeatedly offered to treat me and my companion to gelato and pizza, and we finally accepted on the condition that he allow us to practice discussions with him.

Enzo slowly began to accept the principles of the gospel during our "practice discussions" and make them a part of his life. He came to church and read from the Book of Mormon (or "Book of the Mormons," as he called it). We even spent a memorable afternoon together sitting on a bench overlooking the beautiful Tyrrhenian Sea. As we taught Enzo about the Word of Wisdom, I saw his hand reflexively reach up and cover his shirt pocket with the ever-present, rectangular outline, disclosing a pack of cigarettes. At first, he hesitated. "What does God care if I smoke a few cigarettes a week?" he questioned. As we continued to share our testimonies of the blessings he would receive through obedience to this commandment, Enzo slowly removed the pack of cigarettes and shifted them carefully from hand to hand. When we asked him to commit to following the principles we had shared, his head dropped for a few moments, and then he slowly drew a single cigarette from the full pack and passed it to my companion. He repeated the gesture twice, placing a cigarette in my hand and taking one for himself. Just when I thought he was about to invite us to share in his final smoke, he snapped the cigarette in two and motioned for us to do the same. We took turns breaking all of Enzo's cigarettes. Over the ensuing weeks, his shirt pockets soon lost the familiar outline. Enzo exemplified someone who was ready and willing to deny himself "of all ungodliness, and love God with all [his] might, mind and strength." Though far from perfect, he had started on the path to becoming "perfect in Christ" (Moroni 10:32).

I transferred to a new city a few weeks before his baptismal service but returned to Salerno several times to see his progress. Eventually, Enzo travelled to Bern, Switzerland, to attend the temple and receive his endowment. He also arranged for the temple work to be done for his deceased wife and son. Enzo, his wife, and their only son were sealed in the temple, an eternal family brought into the gospel. When I thought about bringing families into the church, I envisioned a young father and mother standing next to a font, dressed in white and surrounded by several children. Maybe the father would be the next branch president. She could be a Primary president. I certainly didn't picture Enzo Guariglia. I am so grateful I was wrong. Enzo and I continued to stay close through weekly phone calls until his death about ten years after I returned home. I felt blessed to know him. Witnessing his transformation, I can "in nowise deny the power of God" (Moroni 10:32).

Years after my return, I continue to see the fulfillment of mission dreams in unexpected ways. Ten long years after I returned home, the Church broke ground and dedicated a site for the Rome temple. Ten years. The blessing of a temple in Italy did not fit in my perfect mission time line, but just as my MTC teachers had promised, it did come. I learned that being perfect *in* Christ—instead of being perfect *for* Christ—demands patience and faith that promised blessings may not come right away. He promised to "sustain us in our hour of need—and always will, even if we cannot recognize that intervention. Some blessings come soon, some come late, and some don't come until heaven; but for those who embrace the gospel of Jesus Christ, *they come.*[7]

Shortly after I recorded hitting my spiritual rock bottom as a missionary, I began another journal entry:

> As I look back on my mission, I see so many different faces and places. I feel like I must have walked all over this country! I've talked to so many people, looked into so many Italian eyes. I've borne my testimony, invited people to listen to the discussions, come to church, read the Book of Mormon, come to English class, be baptized. I've talked about the Madonna, the Saints, the Pope, the Bible, Padre Pio, Jehovah's Witnesses, Evangelists, miracles, visions. I've felt the influence of the Holy Ghost upon me as I've borne my testimony of Joseph Smith and the Book of Mormon. And I've told these children of God time and time again that God loves them. And who's listened? A handful of people. Whose life has been changed? Mine has.

My personal inadequacies humbled me and taught me that being perfect in Christ looked nothing like my initial vision of perfection.

Throughout my mission, I often reflected on my experience as it compared to the Jaredites from the Book of Mormon. Like my pre-mission self, they had prepared well. I wonder if, as they began their journey, they felt a bit of the naïve overconfidence I felt as I arrived in Italy. (Maybe they saw themselves eating grapes on the beach in the promised land?) But then the storms came, and they were tossed on the waves and buried in the depths of the sea. What a terrifying start to their journey! Were their hearts broken and humbled as mine had been when they accepted this drastically different reality? Based on this scripture, I suspect so: "the wind did never cease to blow towards

---

7 Jeffrey R. Holland, "An High Priest of Good Things to Come," *Ensign,* Nov. 1999.

the promised land. . . . and they did sing praises unto the Lord" (Ether 6:8–9). The storms that appeared to be their greatest trials were the very instruments that brought them to the promised land. Similarly, relinquishing my need for perfection progressed me toward my personal promised land. His grace peeled away my images of black turtlenecks and gelato and revealed a powerful, beloved daughter of God. I shed the burden of perfectionism and invited the power of the Atonement to make me whole—to make me perfect in Christ.

In the end, my favorite mission memory has nothing to do with fashion, composers, buildings, the language, or even baptisms. It is a simple memory, even ordinary. My companion and I spent a summer afternoon in the beautiful garden of Maria Russo, the woman who always supported the missionaries in our branch. She had placed several lemons from her trees on the long, wooden table, along with a knife and small dish of sugar. We hesitated to try them at first, unwilling to embrace the tart citrus shock. Following Maria's lead, we sliced open the lemons, dipped them in sugar and ate them whole, rinds and all, the sticky juices running down our chins. We never imagined that they would taste so satisfying, a perfect combination of sweet and sour. Over the sounds of passing motorini and children playing soccer in the street, Maria chatted with us about the missionaries she had met several years ago. She told us how she had gained a testimony and how the branch and the Lord had supported her through her many health problems. We bore our testimonies and picked a hymn to sing together, Maria's bold voice carrying us all. Rome was, indeed, the perfect mission for me.

MARY JONES SCORESBY hopes to return to Italy for the dedication of the Rome temple. Currently, she stays busy as a wife and mother to four children. Born and raised in Utah, she now considers Bloomington, Indiana, home. She enjoys using her humanities/English degree from BYU to teach, write, or edit whenever possible. Her hobbies are reading and searching for perfect Indian take-out.

Dancing Away Discouragement
Lindsey Stirling

S o the other day, Sister Johanson and I were out tracting in the wealthiest part of our area: Upper Darien. It was a town located right on the border of New Canaan, where every house seemed big enough to support its own zip code. As I gazed at one of the homes, I half expected Miss Scarlet to come running down the driveway looking for Ashley, but alas, that never happened. Instead, we were treated to all of the classically rude responses straight out of Satan's cookbook entitled, "How to Make a Discouraged Missionary." We got them all that night: the door slamming, the mockery, the protective mother who violently pulls her children away from the terrifying twenty-one-year-old girls smiling on her porch. And, my all-time favorite, the woman who looks at us with all the hate of Hades in her eyes as she sternly barks, "I ALREADY HAVE JESUS IN MY LIFE; DON'T COME BACK!"

We had hit almost every house on this giant horseshoe-shaped street, and we'd been emotionally "stoned" at each one of them. In the spirit of enduring to the end, we knocked on the majestic oak entrance of the last house on the street, which was particularly huge. The door opened and I prayed fervently in my heart that this stern-faced old man would soften his heart to our message and . . . PSYCH! Once again we were brutally denied from the last house on the street.

Sister Johanson and I looked at each other, shrugged our shoulders, and began the long trek back to our car. As we began to walk, our gaze fell upon a large field of tall grass and wild-flowers in the middle of the giant semicircular street. "Oh . . . ," Sister Johanson sighed. "I would love to frolic through that field." I smiled mischievously, and seconds later I was running, jumping, and twirling through this field with my companion right on my heels. Every one of the houses from which we had just been rejected had a front-row seat to this frolicking frenzy. I have no doubt that at least a handful of them were peeking through their blinds in confusion, watching two very gleeful disciples whom they had just attempted to crush. We laughed as we turned our faces skyward, threw our arms out, and ran freely through the field. In spite of the rejection we had just experienced, in that moment we felt incredibly happy. It reminded me of a great quote from Jesus Christ himself in Matthew 5:11–12: "Blessed are ye when men shall revile you . . . for my sake. Rejoice, and be exceeding glad: for great is your reward in heaven."

LINDSEY STIRLING is a profes-sional violinist, dancer, choreographer, performing artist, and composer. She has toured 6 continents, perform-ing in nearly 170 cities. Her YouTube channel, from which she gained her popularity (www.youtube.com/lind-seystomp), boasts nearly 4 million sub-scribers, and her debut album has sold almost 250,000 copies. You can "like" Lindsey on Facebook (www.facebook.com/lindseystirlingmusic) or visit her website at www.lindseystirling.com.

Choosing to Serve:
No One Way
Sarah Hogan

"You sisters are crazy to have come on a mission; you don't even have to be here!" The elder in my MTC district clearly spoke for the elders on his left and his right as well. Although they did not say so, their faces suggested that we should seriously consider making a dash for the nearest exit before it was too late.

I was shocked and a little worried. I don't think I really responded. I wondered, *Do these young men think that God has not also called us on a mission?* Certainly, I had no other reason to be there. I had not felt any social or cultural pressure to go. At twenty-four I had only recently begun to think of finding someone to marry. And, although I had grown up with very active LDS parents, I certainly didn't have a proud family history of missionary work. My brother had been the first missionary on both sides of our family to serve a mission in modern times. For my brother's farewell, someone had suggested to my father that he research and tell some stories about our ancestors' missions. My dad discovered that two of our ancestors had served missions: One, a nineteenth century Norwegian immigrant, had traveled back to Norway where he was promptly imprisoned for proselytizing. When he was released a year later, he returned to Utah. The other, an early missionary to the Southern States mission, became so ill that his companions put him on the train with a note pinned to his coat saying his name and which stop they should let him off.

Suffice it to say that when my brother left on his mission as a nineteen-year-old, I, at twenty-one, had never—even in passing—considered that I might serve a mission. In fact, I didn't even attend church at the time. I was studying theater at a small, East Coast liberal arts college where I had encountered narrow-minded unkindness and self-righteousness in my local ward. I decided that I felt a lot happier when I didn't go to church, so I didn't go. Soon, I wasn't sure whether I believed in anything or if I even wanted to.

Upon graduating from college, I got an internship in the costume shop at Princeton University's McCarter Theater. My parents helped me move to New Jersey but held my belongings hostage until we had all visited my "new ward" in Princeton. I didn't bother to protest, but I didn't expect a positive experience. It may have been the fact that several ward members were season ticket holders and seemed to like theater, or simply that I didn't have anything better to do that evening, but for some reason I agreed to go to the young single adult family home evening that night. When they offered a ride for church the next week, I agreed to that too. That autumn, somehow I was at every meeting, activity, or institute class. It wasn't a conscious decision; it just unfolded that way.

I was very lucky to have a boss who made sure I could go to church, even when we worked eighty-hour weeks in the costume shop. I was also blessed to attend church in Princeton with some of the finest Latter-day Saints I have ever known. I made close friends and felt an outpouring of the Spirit that I hadn't realized I had missed so much. As I got to know people in my ward well, I became a part of some extraordinary stories of kindness and generosity. One day, I was thinking about the amazing love I had seen and it occurred to me, *This is what people mean by Christ-like. Christ must be like this!* That was when I first began to feel I knew who He was, through the love that others showed in His name.

I began to read the Book of Mormon and then to pray for someone to read it with me. I felt sure that God would send someone, and soon afterward a young woman appeared. She had just graduated from BYU and found a job nearby and was looking for a place to live. Together, we found an apartment. Lisa had wanted to serve a mission but hadn't felt it was what God wanted for her. Instead, we read the Book of Mormon together every night and she taught me to be excited about general conference. I felt certain that even though a mission had not been in God's plan for Lisa, He had called her to move across the country to New Jersey to help me and many others. When we found it difficult to pay the rent, we advertised for one more roommate and added a lovely non-LDS music student to our nightly scripture study. Our tiny apartment nearly burst with the Spirit.

The theater had offered me a job in the costume shop at the end of my internship, and I'd decided to stay for another year. I wasn't sure about my long-term plans, though. I had wanted to be a costume designer, but now I wasn't sure. I considered pursuing a PhD or joining the Peace Corps. I started praying each night that I would know what I was supposed to do next.

One day it occurred to me that I needed to make a decision about church. I had not attended church when I didn't like my ward, but now that I did like my ward, I was active. What about next time I was in a ward I didn't like? Would I continue to attend church?

A few weeks later, I was lying on the couch in our apartment, thinking, and I realized that I deeply wanted to be a part of God's church. I got up, knelt in the middle of my living room, and promised my Heavenly Father that no matter what, I was committed to doing what He wanted me to do. A beautiful warmth swelled my heart with an invitation to His temple.

I continued to pray about what I should do next, thinking that maybe I'd like to live in California. I'd never been there, but both my roommates were Californians, and it sounded like a fun adventure. One of my friends, who was doing a semester at UC Berkeley, suggested that I fly out to see if I liked it, and I bought a ticket.

As the time of my trip approached though, I became incredibly anxious. California felt so far away. And what if I didn't like it? What would I do with the rest of my life if my only plan fell through? On the eve of my trip, I was so distraught that I considered hiding in my bed all weekend and not telling anyone I hadn't actually gone. I had a thought that I could ask someone for a blessing, but I wasn't sure there was anyone I felt comfortable approaching. One young man came to mind. Troy was a Princeton undergrad who was married to a friend of mine, but then Troy and Crystal were from California. I just couldn't imagine myself explaining that I needed a blessing because I was afraid to go there on vacation.

I had to work that night, and I had some travel books I needed to return to the library, so I forced myself to get out of bed. In the middle of the library, holding the stack of glossy California guidebooks, I ran right into Troy and Crystal. They asked about my trip, and somehow I found myself explaining that I was worried about my looming decisions. During a break from work later that evening I slipped across the street to their student apartment and Troy gave me a blessing. I had only a few minutes, so we didn't talk. Troy asked Crystal to say a prayer. Then he asked my full name and placed his hands on my head.

When Troy began to speak, the heavens opened and the power of God rushed down upon me. I was promised that if I prayed before I left and when I returned, and always remembered to keep a prayer in my heart, I would know what I should do. As soon as he finished speaking, Troy collapsed on the couch, exhausted by the experience. I ran back to the theater beaming with hope. It wasn't that everything suddenly became easy, but everything became possible, because God was there.

The rest of my story sounds almost too simple. I kept praying. I began to experiment with what it meant to keep a prayer always in my heart. I went to California and fell in love with its sunshiny radiance. Then my friend took me to see the Oakland temple. Walking through the gardens, the idea of serving a mission came into my mind, and all the other ideas fell away.

I was called to the Idaho Pocatello Mission. As someone who had never lived west of Pittsburgh, turning over my Friday nights, my entire wardrobe, and my will to the Lord and going to spend a year and a half in Pocatello, Idaho, felt akin to closing my eyes and jumping over the edge of a precipice, trusting God to save me.

With my mission call, I was mailed a card with photos of a mix-and-match wardrobe: navy blazer and straight skirt, subtly patterned floral skirt (both cut exactly to mid-calf), button-down blouse, and navy cardigan. I laughed at the card, but I couldn't help the knot in the bottom of my stomach that said, "You will never be the ideal sister missionary. And do you really want to be?"

In fact, I was a complete foreigner in eastern Idaho, in many ways. I said what I thought. I used too many big words. I made people uncomfortable. I struggled over how to fit in. Then one night I had a terrible cold, and Elder Kearney and Elder Johnson came to give me a blessing. Rules forbade their coming inside our house, and so my companion carried a chair outside. It had already grown dark, and the air was a little chilly. The sky glittered with countless stars. Elder Kearney blessed me with health and then added, "Sister Hogan, your personality is acceptable to the Lord."

For the rest of my mission, I did what I had learned to do in getting my answer to come on a mission. I prayed. And I always kept a prayer in my heart. I relied on God to guide me as I tried to know when to focus on exactness in obedience and when to be myself. As time passed, I discovered that God didn't just need someone to come to Idaho and fit into the mold of a missionary. He had called me because He needed *me*. My insight into why someone might stop coming to church allowed me to help those who struggled. My conviction that those who had strayed from the fold were beloved children of God allowed church leaders and fellow missionaries to see inactive members in a new way. My testimony of the Church inspired members who had never really thought about whether it was true. When President Hinckley clarified that serving a mission was not the right choice for all young women, a few members asked us, "How do you feel, now that President Hinckley said you shouldn't be here?" By then, I knew I should be there.

Missionaries aren't always young men or young women who have always had testimonies or who look like missionaries. They are those who have been called by God to do His work. Shortly after the elders in my MTC district questioned why we were there, I happened upon Acts 2:17–18, "And it shall come to pass in the last days, saith God, I will pour out of my Spirit upon all flesh: and your sons and your daughters shall prophesy, and your young men shall see visions, and your old men shall dream dreams: And on my servants and on my handmaidens I will pour out in those days of my Spirit; and they shall prophesy." Each time I came back to this scripture, I knew that my companions and I were fulfilling ancient prophecy of God's plan for the latter days: that young men and women would be called to bear powerful testimony that He is the Christ.

Because all worthy young women are not required to serve as missionaries, those who do choose to serve have had an opportunity to pray and receive a witness that they have been called of God. For many young women, the decision whether or not to serve a mission is one of their first major life decisions, providing an opportunity to listen not only to the Spirit but also to their own hearts. Here, five women tell their stories about making the decision whether or not to serve a mission.

Elizabeth Tirado

I had always thought that when the time came, I would know whether I should go on a mission. But despite having taken a semester off for humanitarian work in Peru to "figure things out," I had only a vague outline for my future: major in Spanish and then on to law school . . . or maybe culinary school . . . or divinity school . . . or a PhD in Spanish literature? Well, it was more narrowed down than it had been the year before.

Then I realized that my twenty-first birthday was coming up. A mission could be an easy answer to everything. Heavenly Father would tell me I was needed in the mission field, and then, surely, I would come home knowing exactly what I wanted to do in life. I knelt in prayer, ready and willing to receive direction. I fasted that Sunday . . . every Sunday, for three weeks. Why wasn't God telling me what to do?

I sat on the grungy linoleum floor of a galley kitchen in my college apartment, the only place I could find a small corner of peace in a space inhabited by five other girls, and opened my patriarchal blessing. I was hoping to find a passage that I had never noticed before, maybe even floating off the page as if by magic, but instead I found . . . nothing. I closed my eyes and told my Father in Heaven, "I just want to know what *You* want . . ."

Then I heard His response clearly in my mind, "It's not my decision, child. It's yours." I had failed to recognize that I was deciding between two good paths. I took a few more days to explore my feelings, but it didn't take me long to realize my deep desire to serve. The truth of the gospel of Jesus Christ burned in my soul. Sharing my conviction with others seemed the natural progression. Then I went back to the Lord and presented my plan. "I want to serve a mission. As I go about preparing for this, please help me know if it is wrong in any way." I closed my prayer and waited. Peace, calm, and confidence filled my heart and mind. I was supported by the hand of the Lord in every single step of the decision, but it was my decision.

Elizabeth served in the New York New York South Mission, Spanish-speaking, from 2005 to 2007.

Hannah Garcia

My younger brother was out selling pest control in Texas when his mission call arrived in our mailbox in Arizona. We decided that we would open his call on Skype, and I was going to be the one to read it. As I pulled open the white envelope, a thought struck me: *Hey, I want one of these!* It scared me like crazy, and I promptly shoved that thought to a remote corner of my brain. I had never even considered serving a mission, even though I was already twenty-one.

Months later, I was listening to music while driving to my sister's house and just felt an overwhelming joy to be a member of the Church. A simple thought came to me: *I love church music. I could listen to it all day!* From there it escalated. *I could listen to it for a whole week—no, for a whole month! No . . . maybe even eighteen months?* As I continued to drive, I couldn't shake the mission idea. It seemed crazy in one sense, but completely wonderful in another. I thought that maybe Heavenly Father was helping me to realize what my next step was, so I decided to pray about it. Over the following weeks, I prayed and fasted and prayed some more. I went to the temple and sat on the grounds, talked to my bishop, and even made a list of pros and cons. Still, I received no definite answer.

When I talked to my sister about feeling conflicted, she said, "Hannah, sometimes Heavenly Father doesn't give us an answer right away because he wants us to make the choice first." The more I reflected on it, the more it made sense.

One day I sat down and thought about everything that left me feeling conflicted, and then I prayed. I told Heavenly Father that I was going to make a choice, and if He would have me do anything different, I would listen to Him. Then and there I decided that I would go on a mission. A few weeks later, a beautiful confirmation told me I had made the right choice.

Hannah served in the Massachusetts Boston Mission from 2012 to 2013.

Shelley Graham

There was sunshine in my soul one warm autumn day, just a few months before I turned twenty-one. I was headed up to Rock Canyon Park to find a secluded spot high on the mountain to pray. Excited to tell Heavenly Father that I decided to serve a mission, I expected a glorious sacred experience as the Lord confirmed that decision for me.

I knelt to pray and found I couldn't focus. I listened for the Lord's response, "Great job, Shelley! I knew you would make the right choice!" Hallelujah, angels, and so on. But instead I found myself looking for pictures in the clouds. Nature had always been a place for me to study my scriptures and feel close to the Lord.

But now I felt abandoned on a hilltop, frustrated that the Lord wouldn't speak louder than the scrub jays.

For weeks I worried about this. I was sure that my desires were righteous, so I talked with my bishop about it and he counseled me to take my decision to the temple. I made sure that I did everything exactly by the book this time. Just in case the Lord didn't like how I made the mountain my metaphorical temple, I was going to the real temple this time. I went in fasting and prayer, knowing this time I would hear the hallelujah and the angels. Instead, it was painfully silent—not the peaceful, leaving-the-world-behind kind of quiet, but a straining-to-hear-anything-but-the-sweet-little-sister-playing-the-organ kind of quiet.

I wrote in my journal:

> I don't know what I'm doing wrong—what I'm leaving out in this process of finding an answer. I told the Lord that I would be willing to leave school and my family to serve Him. I listened so hard for anything the Lord might say—for almost twenty minutes. I sat in the baptistry, listening, and I felt nothing. I felt like a spiritual failure. . . . What do I do now? I have no idea how to continue. Do I keep praying about this?

My parents gently suggested that perhaps I wasn't willing to recognize an answer I didn't want. I was dumbfounded. It never occurred to me that all of this constituted one grand stupor of thought. I struggled in letting go of the idea of a mission. I couldn't understand why such a righteous desire wouldn't be in the Lord's plan for my life. I wanted all of the experiences of a mission: the hard work, devotion, and gospel study. And now I worried that I would always feel cheated in some way.

Looking back over the fifteen years since that decision, I am grateful for every step my life has taken, even those that took me away from a formal mission. I have had numerous chances to learn hard work, to improve my personal gospel study, and to devote myself to small groups of people—students, young women, Relief Society sisters, and my family. I know now that part of my life's mission is finding ways to share the gospel every day, and it sometimes requires a little extra creativity. But I look forward to serving a formal mission later in life, and I love this life the Lord has given me. In the stillness of my living room, just before the sunlight taps the mountains (and not long before my home erupts in quick bare feet, tattered blankies, and cold cereal) I feel certain that I made the right choice.

Shortly after this experience, Shelley went on to finish her BFA and MFA at BYU.

Katie Sidwell

The moment he finished popping the question, my visions of me in a mid-calf beige skirt for the next eighteen months morphed into a full-length, form-fitting Vera Wang wedding gown. Mission or marriage? In one hand, I had an unopened mission call and in the other, a wedding ring.

Choosing between two things I had wanted so badly my entire life paralyzed me. To a girl whose indecision resulted in agonizingly long trips to the grocery store trying to pick the best water bottle, I felt completely overwhelmed making such a weighty decision on my own. This was no water bottle. When I received my patriarchal blessing in high school, it spoke of people being prepared for my arrival. It said Heavenly Father was asking me to participate in His work if I chose to do so. From that, it seemed clear that Heavenly Father wanted me to serve; the problem was, I didn't really want to serve a mission, at least not then. And the phrase, "If you so choose . . ." left a little back door escape.

On to college I went, a small part of me dreaming about the perfect man I would hopefully meet my freshman year. I didn't.

But, the fall of my junior year, I met him—the man who embodied all the qualities I'd wanted in a husband. At first our relationship was fun and frivolous but as the months went on, it turned more stressed and serious. My birthday loomed, but neither of us knew what I would decide concerning a mission.

After weeks of pondering, praying, and fasting for an answer, I realized a piece of my heart was hoping I would get the answer to stay home. It was the easiest and most logical solution. Why put off the life I sorely wanted when it was right here before me, free for the taking? I went to my parents pleading for guidance. My dad's response rocked me: "You may regret not going, but you will never regret going." Peace surrounded my heart, and I immediately felt clear-minded. The unknown changed from scary to exciting. I wanted to serve. I wanted to go to the people awaiting my arrival and use my testimony as an instrument of conversion. No matter how many different ways I tried to rationalize and justify why it was the best decision for me to marry this boy, I could not feel peace about it. I had to tell him no. With this rush of the Spirit, my heart was ready to accept that I had made the right decision.

When I arrived in Madrid, I set my bags down and gazed out the window overlooking the temple. In that quiet moment, the Spirit completely engulfed me and confirmed that yes, this was absolutely the right decision. I was exactly where the Lord wanted me to be. I was exactly where I wanted to be. I knew with my whole heart that not only had I made the best decision, but also that I had made my own decision.

My mission molded me into the person I truly wanted to be but couldn't become on my own. I saw those who had been prepared to receive the gospel, like my patriarchal blessing said, and my joy was full as I helped them come to Christ. Even now, years later,

I continue to receive blessings in my life because of my service. My deeply sacred experiences gave me a clarified view of eternity.

While at one point, the decision between mission and marriage felt so final, I later realized it really wasn't. I did not give up the life I had always wanted. Several years after coming home, I met the man—the one I always assumed didn't really exist—and married him in the temple. Deciding to serve a mission was grueling. The mission itself was demanding, but my dad was right. I will never regret having served a mission for the Savior. I am proud of the choice I made.

Katie served in the Spain Madrid Mission from 2003 to 2004.

Sydney Arvanitas

The process I endured in deciding to serve a mission certainly wasn't an easy one. As President Monson made the announcement, I, like so many other girls that day, saw myself as a missionary. I experienced a jolt of joy and peace and . . . understanding. For a brief moment, I knew that I would serve a mission. In that moment, I wanted to serve a mission—for myself, for my future family, and for those waiting to hear the glorious message of the gospel.

Doubt slowly crept into my mind in the weeks that followed. I began to question whether what I felt that day was real or just the adrenaline rush of witnessing history firsthand. I knew only one thing for certain—I could not commit to a mission unless I was absolutely sure. I didn't want to be the missionary who realizes what she's gotten herself into once it's too late.

It was a question I agonized over, one that kept me up worrying night after night. I couldn't understand why Heavenly Father was refusing to give me a straight answer. Finally, I could stand it no longer. I decided that my prayers could only be answered if I exercised faith and made the decision on my own, praying for confirmation. At first, nothing happened. Although terrified of not getting an answer, I resolved to carry on. One night, as I was studying my scriptures I came across the verse in the Doctrine and Covenants that reads, "Did I not speak peace to your mind concerning the matter? What greater witness can you have than from God?" (D&C 6:23). There was my answer. After months of confusion, Heavenly Father helped me to recognize that the peace I had felt in the moment the announcement was made had been real and right, and that it truly had been a revelation from Him.

Sydney Arvanitas is currently serving in the Korea Taejon Mission.

For each of us women in this chapter, the decision about a mission was more than just a yes or no about being a missionary. It was an opportunity to see ourselves as daughters of God and to learn to follow the Spirit as we tried to see who He wanted us to become. At the same time, the decision needed to be ours. Whether the answer for us individually was to serve a mission or to serve at home, the confidence we gained as we learned to seek God has blessed our lives. Our experiences have become a part of the women we are today.

SARAH HOGAN earned an MA in education at Harvard University and now applies her proselyting skills to convincing her ESL students to read more often. She and her husband have two children (four and eight years old) who beg her to write pretend mission calls for them and then let them knock on her door.

The First Three Months:
Diary of a Greenie
Jen Nuckols

Tuesday, July 16, 2002

Sister Nuckols has embarked! My time at the CTM[8] has ended, and I am about "to missionary" as soon as this plane lands in João Pessoa. Holy excitement! I'm not nervous or worried or sad, just peaceful and ready. I already miss my two great CTM companions, but in a few hours, I will have a mission president, a companion, and an area. I have felt the burning power of the Holy Ghost confirm to me the reality of the existence of God, of the Savior, of the Book of Mormon. It is all true! I love it and am privileged to be a part of it.

Thursday, July 18, 2002

Oh my gosh! This is so hard. I'm in shock. I've been all teary these last two days. I cried last night when I was going to bed and again when Sister Santos (another missionary in my house) asked if there was anything she could do to help me. This morning, I did a good job holding it in until I got into the shower, but when the cold water hit the back of my neck, I sobbed. Later, I had to say a prayer at the home of one of our investigators, and as soon as I said, "*Pai Celestial*" (Heavenly Father), I lost it. I felt the Spirit a

---

8 Centro de Treinamento Missionário, the MTC in São Paulo, Brazil.

50

lot while we were teaching, but as soon as we would walk outside into the street, I would start to cry again.

What am I doing here?! There was one good hour today in the middle of the afternoon when I was able to focus and get some memorizing done (I have to get all these discussions passed off!) but for the most part, I have been walking around in a shocked daze. Yesterday the excitement from the airport wore off, and I didn't even have the desire to go out and contact and it was my FIRST day! My companion, Sister W., does not like tracting or contacting people, and I think that we spent too much time visiting members. The hours between 2 p.m., when lunch ends, and 9:30 p.m., when we go home, seem SO LONG especially because we do not have things scheduled.

This is a bigger sacrifice than I ever realized before. A year seems impossibly long, not to mention sixteen more months.

Friday, July 19, 2002

I had a good cry today at lunch and let it all out. What if this emotional overload is just PMS? Sometimes it seems like I'm watching a movie of someone else's life, because this does not feel like my reality. When the Lord asks us to sacrifice all that we have and all that we are, He was not asking for a little. This is the big time! I really feel the magnitude of this sacrifice. I don't even have time to explore or enjoy the culture because it's all about teach, teach, teach. I can't really imagine this level of intensity for sixteen more months: an endless Sabbath!

Saturday, July 20, 2002

I've been praying so much during free time that I have hardly been working on memorizing at all. I've needed so much help! I've especially needed help controlling my thoughts and keeping them focused on people here, and not elsewhere, or on other people from other parts of my life.

Tuesday, July 23, 2002

My first zone meeting left me in tears. The whole thing was just so discouraging. Once again, it seemed like I was watching a movie of someone else's life. We walked in and found the elders wrestling each other in the gym, and then once the meeting started, I had a hard time understanding them as they shared tactics about how to find more men to teach. The gathering also made me feel isolated and unknown: I'm really not part of this group yet, of this culture of the João Pessoa mission.

We walked all the way back to our area from the zone meeting, and then we walked even farther to our lunch appointment. I'm grateful that I felt divine strength sustaining me when I really should not have been able to walk anymore. Later in the day, Sister W. and I stopped at a member's home to set up an appointment with her, and she made us fried meat cakes and put church music on in the background. As I shared my little message with her from 3 Nephi 11:15, I felt the strength of the Spirit and the strength of that woman. She nourished us both physically and spiritually.

Thursday, July 25, 2002

The time has come to cast off homesickness, CTM companionship withdrawal, and regular morning tears. Buck up! I really want to love being a missionary, and right now I do not, so I will just start. Sure, a year and a half seems long—oh shoot, why am I tearing up again?—but this is just how it's going to be, and I'm gonna like it! The time has come to put heart, might, mind, and strength into this work and to stop feeling sorry for myself. Father,

I already love the country, the language, and the culture; please help me to love the work!

One thing that helps me is to think of other sister missionaries I have known who did this. They say that they loved every minute, and my guy friends have said the same thing, but is that really true?! I'm sure that they had challenges and other things that grated on them, but I guess that did not override their overall sense of peace and joy in serving. I wonder if I will ever feel that.

I feel that I have great potential as a missionary. I know that I am capable of doing great things with the Lord's help. I just need to get over this transition phase.

Saturday, July 27, 2002

Mornings are so hard for me, even after a previous day of successful work. Possible explanations: cold shower, having too much time to think, and eating Special K with strawberries that reminds me of home (which came in a care package that I just got from Mom).

Monday, August 5, 2002

I feel better right now than I have since I arrived in the field. God answers fasts and prayers. Last night, I still felt down, but tonight, after a very relaxing P-day, I was on fire. I felt physically energized and was excited to visit with people. Portuguese wasn't going to hold me back tonight! During our last appointment, we taught Juliana, her sister, and her brother. They all seem so sincere, and the older sister, in particular, really wants to know the truth. I felt the excitement and enthusiasm of the Spirit as we taught. Over the past few weeks, I have prayed for other people, but I have not had the urgent desire, as I do now. I love these girls and desire for them to be baptized. Father, thank you for giving me this vision and excitement!

Tuesday, August 6, 2002

Ups and downs. Today I never shook off my morning fog. We walked for two and a half hours this morning, clapped at doors, waited, then walked some more; we must have crossed our entire area ten times! Now I'm sunburned, my feet are blistered, and I almost fell asleep while walking. Then I really did fall asleep for a second (or a minute?) while Sister W. was teaching and I was sitting in a plastic rocking chair.

Saturday, August 10, 2002

The night before last, I had my first dream about the mission. I am excited that my subconscious has finally arrived here too. I dreamed that Juliana and her siblings got baptized. Joy, sweet joy!

Monday, August 12, 2002

Sister W. and I are not very good friends. We go about our labors peacefully, but we rarely laugh together, and I don't feel any sort of emotional bond. Sometimes I fear that I am subtly mean to her—or at least I'm not as loving and supportive as I should be.

Tuesday, August 13, 2002

I have been craving the call to be a missionary for twenty-one years, and when I finally arrive, I'm depressed. Mostly, I feel unworthy, insufficient, and inadequate. Heavenly Father, what is wrong with me?

Wednesday, August 14, 2002

For some reason the Lord has seen fit for me to experience this time of homesickness/drudgery/sadness, but He has told me through my patriarchal blessing to be patient and my mission will be all that I want it to be: a time of hard work and JOY!

Wednesday, August 21, 2002

Bipolarity! Yesterday was euphoria. Today, not so much.

Thursday, August 22, 2002

In her letter, Grame told me to "take time for myself" in order to preserve my skin: a comical statement in its illogicality and improbability.

I felt the Lord use me to communicate His love to the woman who fed us lunch. She was the first member who fed me in the field, and I remember feeling touched that first day by the way she presented her humble meal and said, "I prepared this with my heart." This time, I shared Doctrine and Covenants 4:2 with her and told her that she is indeed serving with her heart. I was moved by the Spirit and by the fact that God would use me in that way.

Tuesday, August 27, 2002

I'm living a completely different mission! I just received the best possible gift of a companion, a Brazilian, Sister H. During the past thirty-six hours since her arrival, my feelings, my work, and my missionary life have taken a one hundred eighty-degree turn. Not only does she have incredible people skills, missionary techniques, and work ethic, she is also already my friend. Here are some of the little changes that make a huge difference:

- She loves making contacts and she stops people on the street without hesitation.
- She has me keep a planner so that we both write down names, addresses, and appointments. I am now a more active participant in my daily activities.
- We bear testimony to each other in the morning before we pray.

- We sit down at night to discuss the day's outcome and our strategy for tomorrow. Now I have something specific to anticipate instead of street wanderings.
- She's not too cheap to take the bus to and from zone meeting so that we gain more work time in our area; we don't just try to kill time until lunch or until the next appointment.
- She encourages me, constantly asking my opinion and offering productive tips.

I do not want my well-being in the mission to be dependent on my companions, and I never blamed my adjustment misery on my trainer, but these sisters do really have a huge impact on me, especially as a new, unknowledgeable missionary. I am so grateful and excited for all the days to come with Sister H.

On P-day eve we had a feast of scrambled eggs, fresh biscuits, chocolate sauce, and watermelon. What a funny life this is!

Thursday, August 29, 2002

Image of the day: sprinting through a field of sand at 11 a.m. to try to teach at least one discussion before lunch. Everything else we had scheduled for the morning had fallen through. The sensation of running in search of a teaching opportunity starkly differed from standing in the street, clueless, unsure where to go next.

Yesterday after lunch, as we lay on our beds in a tired stupor, I asked Sister H. what she was thinking. She responded that she was thinking about the upcoming ward activity that we were in charge of, how it would come together, and who we would take with us. I had been thinking about how long I have been in the mission (only six weeks!) and how much time I have left. I am acutely aware of TIME here but I do not want to be. Sister H.'s positive influence is great, but, Father, I still need Thy help in just being present here!

Friday, September 6, 2002

Pure Brazil! Capoeria is stunning. We stumbled onto a class tonight to find capoeiristas dressed in white, swinging and kicking to the beat of the berimbaus. At the end, they broke into samba. It was so beautiful! It was as if I were watching a show for tourists, but no, it was real. This is pure, undefiled culture—real Brazilian life!

Thursday, September 12, 2002

My face is simultaneously oozing and pulsating. Mosquito bites combined with a rash, an inflamed eye, and a zit breakout, make for a horrifying face. I was in pain and discouraged most of the day. I think that the swelling might be a mango allergy. But mangoes are one of my favorite things about Brazil right now!

Thursday, September 26, 2002

I can't believe how many inactives we encounter! It's a rare miracle to find people who are truly converted or who even want to be converted. I can empathize with Christ crying over the city of Jerusalem, and I stand in awe of what the prophet and apostles must feel when they look at the Church as a whole.

Tuesday, October 8, 2002

I cried when the closing prayer ended the final session of general conference. I didn't want those leaders—and even the members of the Tabernacle Choir—to leave and go back to their homes: I wanted them to stay with me and be my friends and support me.

One of the best parts of conference was the attendance of many recent converts: Emerson (who said it was his best Saturday ever!), Rajeane, Fatima, and Senhor Aldymar, who isn't even baptized yet. I'm so happy that they were able to feel the power of the words of the prophets and to see the magnitude of what they are now a part of. I ache for them to have more spiritual experiences to strengthen their conversion.

Friday, October 11, 2002

Sometimes out of nowhere comes a clear, yet random image from home. These images have included the aisle in Sam's Club where they sell the Mach 3 razors, the parking lot and entrance to Macaroni Grill, the streets of Manhattan (which I have only visited once), and the entrance to the public library parking lot. These memories strike me in all their vibrancy at the most random times. Sometimes I think I harbor them because they are comfortable, familiar, unattainable. But glorifying them makes the current moment less desirable, which is not what I want. During my first three years of college, or traveling in Asia or even in the CTM, images of home would never attack me in this way; I never thought longings for home would be a problem for me. But they are keeping me from a more powerful immersion in the work. Father, I will do my part to not foster or give root to these thoughts. Even though it feels like letting go of my blanky (or favorite dolly or binky), I will do it in order to be free.

Tuesday, October 15, 2002 a.m.

I am no longer the newest American sister in the mission! Sister A. has arrived and I met her this morning at zone meeting. She is sharp and eager and had a terrible first week. I related to everything she said and wanted to shake her and hug her and tell her, "Yes, it's tough, but it gets better."

Tuesday, October 15, 2002 p.m.

This morning I covered my hair with baby powder to absorb the grease: there was no running water! Last night I slept in my sweat from that day and now it's layered with today's sweat. We offered a prayer for water and it came, as we asked, before 10 p.m. It ran out, however, while I was still covered with soap.

Thursday, October 17, 2002

I am grateful for great days, as was yesterday. The Spirit was tangible and powerful in the discussions, in the streets, in our hearts. My heart kept crying out, "I love doing this!"

Saturday, October 19, 2002

Tonight I felt like a missionary! Neither companionship had an appointment tonight, so we joined forces and spent the evening singing hymns and passing out contact cards in a little hospital and in two public squares. To stand up in public and verbalize my testimony through both word and music is truly a missionary's privilege.

Fourteen Months Later . . .

Friday, December 12, 2003

Heavenly Father is being so kind and generous to me in my last week of my mission. For four days in a row, I have felt only pure peace, calm, joy, rejoicing, spirit, love, friendship. I feel grateful for the past and hopeful for the future. I feel the Lord magnifying my ability to love and my capacity to feel peace and joy. I don't have any worries, afterthoughts, stress, pressure, or concerns. *Só alegria!* (Only joy!)

Monday, December 15, 2003

I'm almost home! I'm on the last leg of the flight from Atlanta to San Diego. The first time it hit me that I was really going home was when I went through customs in São Paulo. The Brazilian customs officer asked if I was ever coming back, and I said no and started to weep. He became all uncomfortable. When I asked him if I could take my homemade coconut cake with me, he said no problem.

I cried when the plane took off in São Paulo and when I arrived at the Atlanta airport and felt totally alone and out of place. Even though I was technically back in my own country, I felt like an outsider. I was the only one wearing sandals and a summer dress! To my joy, I found a Brazilian young man who had been on my flight, and we spoke Portuguese together. It felt so natural and comfortable. Speaking to him made me feel at home. Oh, how I'm going to miss it.

JEN NUCKOLS is a writer and mental health and addictions counselor in Seattle. An avid adventurer, she has cycled down the West Coast, summited Mt. Rainier, taught in the South Bronx, and advocated for the empowerment of women in Africa.
A graduate of Stanford and the University of Washington, she pursues her passion for travel, social justice, and Brazil by chasing the World Cup to wherever that may lead her.

Shield-Bearing Sister
Elise Babbel Hahl

I couldn't see anything dangerous about the man approaching us, not at first. "May I speak with you two?" he asked, as he wobbled to a stop on his bike. He looked first to Sister Lima[9] and then to me, from my name tag down to my sandals.

"Yes," I said, and he stepped off his bike onto the dirt road. I extended my hand to shake his. In my seven months of experience, a person who would approach a pair of sister missionaries of his own volition was probably a teenage boy on a dare, a Jehovah's Witness trying to stump us, an old drunk, or every so often, a golden investigator. We didn't always know which person we were dealing with at first. I hardly noticed the way this particular man slurred his words together because everyone in town seemed to run their words together in a slow, backwater drawl. We were working on a tiny dot on the map in the middle of the Brazilian Amazon, a four-hour bus ride away from the nearest city. Even the locals called their home "the end of the universe." Here, where the phones and faucets stopped working for a few hours each day, there was never much of a reason to talk fast.

The man inched toward me and started to speak, making broad gesticulations in the air. I didn't want to back away because I thought I'd offend him when the situation was probably harmless.

9 Name changed.

61

It was still light outside, and people were bustling all around us. But when the man looked away for a second, Sister Lima extended her arm and forced me behind her. She narrowed her eyes at me and then turned to him.

"We'll talk to you another time when we don't have an appointment to go to," she told him. "Thanks." And then she practically pushed me away from him and into the street, where the *interiores*—country dwellers—walked along the main dirt road, heading home after a long day of selling fish or eggs. The occasional policeman on a motorbike buzzed by us.

"What was that about?" I asked.

"Don't be stupid."

"You overreacted," I said.

"You need to back away when men get close. You never do that!"

A low blow, if I had ever heard one. "You think I wanted his attention?" I said. "I was trying to be polite! He said he wanted to talk to us."

"You really are foolish, but at least you can always depend on me to protect you from danger."

Nice, I thought. *I'm working with the Pink Power Ranger.* Sister Lima came up only to my nose and was several pounds lighter than me. She was a fiery redhead from southern Brazil who had years of training in Jiu Jitsu, which somehow empowered her to treat me as a protectorate. We did attract a lot of attention because of our pale skin and lighter-than-normal hair, but I never thought we'd have any trouble. Not in a town where the main event seemed to be kite-flying on Sunday evening. I knew better than to frustrate Sister Lima by laughing, so I nodded gravely and made fun of the whole thing in my journal that night instead.

I did a lot to disappoint Sister Lima, or SL, as I referred to her in my journal. We had first met at a zone conference near the beginning of my mission. She and her companion at the time had parked themselves in different corners of the room, both crying. I was concentrating on the food from the buffet table when she approached me. "Will you go with me to speak to *Presidente?*" she asked. I nodded and left my plate behind, and then we walked into another room to speak with the mission president privately. As soon as we had the space to ourselves, she rattled off a list of grievances—at least, that's what I thought she was doing. I liked my Portuguese at a slow deliberate pace, preferably in a Gringo accent, but her words seemed to come out in cartwheels and handsprings, flips and twists. The tumbling grew more and more frantic, her voice higher and higher, and I felt more and more baffled, until her voice cracked and she began to weep. Routine over. The mission president looked sympathetic, but he didn't have much to say in response, which led me to wonder how often she had that kind of talk with him.

She left the conversation believing that I, who had stood there like a traffic cone, was delicate and sweet. From then on, unbeknownst to me, she began praying that one day we might be assigned to be companions.

Her prayer was answered a few months later when the mission president sent the two of us on a long, bumpy bus ride through the jungle to a town I couldn't pronounce, where we were assigned to work together until further notice. She learned quickly that I wasn't quite what she had ordered. Just a few weeks into our companionship, she cornered me. "You look like my little sister," she said, "and I thought you were going to be tender and vulnerable, like her." Her brown eyes narrowed. "But you're not like my sister," she said. "You are *dura.*" That meant I was hard, stubborn, or thick-skulled.

She had a point. As a junior companion who was supposed to follow her lead, I was far too opinionated. I would tell her, for example, "I don't think we should spend a lot of time eating pancakes at a member's house today. We should be finding people who want to hear the discussions instead."

And she'd say, "But these people invited us. They want our support." And then the inevitable, "Where is your heart?"

And then I'd say, "We're wasting our time! We should be out knocking on doors, at the very least."

And then she'd say, "That never works! None of your plans do. If you had my experience on the mission, you would understand."

"Well, I think we should at least try."

"Thanks for the advice, senior." That meant that I was being insubordinate.

Sister Lima loved to clean the house on preparation day. All day. Everywhere. She emulated her mother, who taught her from a young age to keep a spanking clean home. I emulated my mother too, but I couldn't remember her scrubbing out the freezer on a weekly basis.

"Why don't you clean the bathroom today?" she'd ask me the morning of our preparation day. I was always a little reluctant to leave my letter writing, but I knew I had to help, so I'd go and scrub the floor tiles for half an hour until everything looked clean. SL, inevitably, would come inspect. "Did you really clean this for half an hour? There are soap scum spots on this floor!" I looked a little closer at the floor. Yes, those did look like spots. "Don't you know anything?" she'd say. "You're supposed to wipe the floor this way."

Later, she wrote a letter to my mother and told her that I needed some work, but that she was going to teach me how to clean to prepare me for my future husband and children. I was furious. And I couldn't believe my mother's reply. She wrote back, "Thank you for helping our daughter," she wrote. "She is so messy!"

I was able to come to terms with that mother of mine on my official Mother's Day phone call. On the second Sunday in May, we walked into the ward building after everyone had left, and I was able to sit in a small, boxlike office by myself as I caught up with my family over the phone. I swiveled back and forth in the chair as I learned about my little brother's latest mile time and my little sister's eye surgery. I was really just thrilled to be alone for once. Everyone seemed proud of me. There was no conflict, no tension in my stomach. After ninety minutes, I hung up the phone, satisfied.

SL took my spot in the swivel chair after I hung up. She was the only member of the Church in her family, and her mother hardly ever her wrote letters or emails, so this phone call was sacred. Even though her mother didn't understand or support the idea of a mission, Sister Lima admired her fiercely. I sat on the floor outside the office to read while she began her phone conversation. From my spot, I could hear Sister Lima's muffled Portuguese, and once again, the words began to tumble out of her mouth faster and faster and higher and higher. Her voice started to quaver. After less than twenty minutes, she hung up, turned off the light, and hurried out of the office. I followed her out of the church building, dying to know what had happened on the phone call. What could have gone wrong? Had she told her mother what a stubborn companion I was? Was she complaining about my bathroom-cleaning skills? We walked all the way home in the dark without her uttering a word, but as soon as we opened the door to our house, she collapsed on the floor and wept.

After a few unsure moments, I knelt down and put my hand

on her back. She turned around and looked at me, tears running down her face. "My mother yelled at me," she said, "because I called collect."

The following preparation day, Sister Lima seemed to find everything that I was doing wrong. I was misguided, my parents were misguided, she couldn't wait to be transferred away from me . . . over and over. I didn't like feeling attacked, so I tried to ignore her and write letters on my own. At the end of the day, she confronted me in our dining room in a cold, calm voice: "You may be wondering why I've been treating you this way today," she said. Why, yes, I was. "I've actually been testing you."

"What?"

"I wanted to know if you really cared about me. That's why I tested you," she said.

I couldn't believe this. What was going on? Was this a normal missionary thing in the Amazon? Like *Survivor*? I was suddenly curious to know how I scored.

"Sister, you failed," she said solemnly. "It's clear that you don't really care about me."

I wanted to protest her conclusion, but I didn't know what to say. In the end, I was afraid that she was right.

About a week later, the real test came for our companionship. We walked out of the house for our morning appointment and Sister Lima told me she had a dream the night before: "We were walking outside and a man came up to us. He wanted to kill you, but you had no idea. You were acting really ditsy, so it was up to me to save you." We both laughed. Even in her dreams, she was trying to protect me from bad guys. It was nice to forget the way we had treated each other before and feel like friends, at least for a while.

Later that day, my voice grew hoarse because of a cold. I seemed to get them all the time from shaking too many hands, even in the summer. By evening time, Sister Lima was doing all the talking herself because when I opened my mouth, nothing came out. That was probably a nice break for her.

That night we taught a family and I tried to stay engaged, even though I couldn't do much more than nod and smile. When the visit was over, we walked away on a dirt road, with a thick wall of forest on the left side and a few crossroads on the right. It was half past eight—too dark by then to see the green and gold of the flags that lined the streets in celebration of the World Cup. They had changed into jagged shadows. As usual, there was no distant rumble from any trains, planes, or buses. The lights from the high school fell far behind us as we walked, and our road grew darker.

We made our way down the deserted road for a minute or two, and then we heard someone behind us on a bicycle. He passed us and then circled around to a stop. "Can I talk to you?" he asked us. SL hardly looked up before she said yes. He stepped off his bike and asked her to hold it for him. She let him place the handlebars in her palms and looked away for a second, as if she were bored. Another weird street conversation, she was probably thinking. Where did these people come from? The man, now free from his bike, started to inch toward me. It had been too dark to see him clearly when he first approached us, but as he drew nearer I could see something wrapped around his face—something that looked like a black T-shirt. The only features I could make out were his two bloodshot eyes, illuminated by the distant lights of the high school. He came closer toward me, his eyes never leaving mine. I didn't extend my hand for a handshake, as I usually did. I stepped back as he stepped toward me. Something was wrong. Something was off. I tried to think of how to get out of the situation politely.

Without saying a word, the man pulled something shiny out

of his pocket in a slow, stealthy motion. Even though my voice had been gone all day, I screamed—I screamed so loud that I hardly knew it was my own voice. He said nothing. He just gripped the knife in his right hand and pushed it closer to me until it was nearly touching the fabric of my dress. I felt as if I were watching a movie of him moving in closer and me standing there, motionless.

Without a word, Sister Lima shoved the bike onto our attacker. She grabbed my hand, and suddenly my legs could move again. We turned and ran away from him. When I finally had the courage to look back, I saw him in the exact same spot, watching us run.

We ran left onto a street with a few well-lit homes, where a kindly middle-aged couple let us into their home. They allowed us to sit down and use their phone, and they even made some herbal tea for us. We were able to wait there, at turns calm and crying, until a man from our ward came to walk us back home. We couldn't identify our attacker the next day at the police station, but I can still picture his silhouette on the street, a T-shirt draped around his head and his hands gripping the bike.

When I think of that night, I think of an earlier night spent in the secluded safety of my own hometown—the night I was set apart to be a missionary. A member of the stake presidency gave me a beautiful blessing, but afterward, my father told me privately that he felt prompted to give me an additional priesthood blessing. When we arrived home, he laid his hands upon my head and blessed me that I would be protected on my mission, in one of the more moving spiritual experiences I had had up to that point.

The Lord said that He would be a "shield" to His messengers (D&C 35:14), and I had felt the power of that protection firsthand.

What surprised me though was that one of the shield-bearers protecting me was my very own fiery, redheaded companion. The same person who had been a puzzle to me five minutes earlier was the one who had the cool head and confidence to help us escape and the dream that turned out to be prophetic. In the end, I dearly needed my companion.

I realized that my occasional fantasy to be a missionary in my own independent, untethered way was actually a horrible idea. Without a companion, not only would I never correct the things about myself that needed changing, I would be left to survive—or not—on my own. The experience helped me to understand that companionship wasn't just some quirky side-aspect of missionary work. Preaching the word "in the mouths of two or three witnesses" (2 Corinthians 13:1) was central to our purposes because it allowed us to give each other spiritual and physical support.

Sister Lima and I were promptly transferred out of the area. We were reassigned to what was probably the safest area in all of Brazil, a suburb straight out of "Leave It to Beaver," with gates, paved streets, and lots of streetlights. We got good at retelling our story to the other missionaries, none of whom had experienced anything like this. A few elders even said, "I wish that had happened to me!" Right. Sister Lima and I worked in our new area for two months and then left for different areas and companions. She went home shortly afterward, having completed her mission, and I didn't expect to ever see her again.

Nearly two years later, I had gone home, graduated from college, married, and returned to Brazil with my husband. We had both found jobs that allowed us to work in São Paulo, and I was excited to use my Portuguese again. One of our favorite things to do while we were there was to attend the São Paulo temple. It was there one night, while I was whispering to my husband in the chapel before a session, that I noticed a familiar redhead sitting behind me.

I don't know whose jaw dropped lower, hers or mine.

"I don't believe it!" she said. We laughed and I embraced her, this companion of mine who had seen me through the darkest night of my life. I felt as if I had found a long-lost family member. There was no straining, no resentment. It reminded me of the way I've always imagined the reunion between Ammon and Alma after the mission, when Ammon's joy was "so great even that he was full; yea, he was swallowed up in the joy of his God" (Alma 27:17). I wish I could have known on my mission what it would feel like to see her afterward—how little I would care about our squabbles about the best way to proselyte and to clean the bathroom floor. I wish that I hadn't wasted time suspecting her motives before the attack put her in a new light—that I could have perceived that she was the only one in that small town in the Amazon who really supported me and cared about me, simply because she was my companion. I wish I could have known that I would one day love her. For that matter, I wish that every missionary who ever struggled with a companion could conceive that they'd one day rejoice to see that person again, after time spent together in the service of the Savior.

We could hardly keep our voices to whispers as I introduced her to my husband, who thanked her for allowing me to stay alive so that he could marry me. SL smiled. We made plans to do things that we could never do on our mission—mall cruising and lunch at a restaurant.

The next day, I picked up Sister Lima on the way to the mall. We chatted about her husband and family, who were back home for the weekend. She seemed serene in a way that she hadn't been on the mission. It seemed so natural that she was sitting in the passenger seat and talking to me like a real friend. She was the one person on my mission who wasn't afraid to tell me I needed work, the only one who could name all my weaknesses and faults but who still wanted to protect me—like a sister.

"Are you trying to kill us?" she cried as I cut in front of the car in the other lane. It was a little trick I had learned while driving in São Paulo. "In the United States, don't they make you take a driving test before you get your license?" she asked me.

Exactly like a sister.

ELISE BABBEL HAHL studied English at Stanford University and went on to earn a master's degree in nonfiction writing at Johns Hopkins University. Most recently, her work was published in *Choosing Motherhood*, another compilation that she edited. Elise lives with her husband (and former mission pen pal), Oliver, and their four children. She has never gotten over her craving for *pão de queijo* (cheese bread), her favorite Brazilian snack.

Run and Not Be Weary
Dawn Wessman

There is a secret all sister missionaries know.

Are you ready? Here it is:

Physically, missions are hard. Like, crazy, tiring, I-want-to-sleep-for-three-years-after-I-get-home hard. They are more physically and spiritually demanding, and more emotionally depleting than most anything you can experience.

Eve, Sariah, the Israelite women, and every pioneer woman knew this same truth: the Lord often asks his servants to do and be things that require a lot of physical energy. These callings can last for what feels like a long time—forty years in the wilderness, eighteen years raising a child, or eighteen months in Russia.

But the secret is two-part!

Here is the other half:

Christ shares his physical strength with the women doing His work! This physical enabling power is called *Grace*. It is Christ's strength pulsing through your veins. And His power can be with you on your mission, whether that mission is mothering, schooling, or formally preaching the restored gospel as a full-time missionary.

It only took me a full year of knocking my head against the wall in Russia to figure this out. I was called to a mission whose name I mispronounced for the first six months. Located just above Siberia on the Ural Mountains, it was wicked, I-stepped-over-a-frozen-body-on-the-way-to-district-meeting cold. Yes, it was that cold.

We walked a lot. Most companionships lived miles away from the nearest experienced adult leader of the Church. We were entrusted to navigate these cities alone, hunting for those in search of truth. My companions and the people we met warmed my soul, despite the cold weather. I found family and friends on the icy tundra.

But I had a weakness (one of many): In my attempt to be a valiant, hard-working missionary, I wanted to be able to log whatever tracting hours those darn elders were logging.

I had a pride problem. And it was making me physically sick.

I got the incorrect notion in my head that a truly valiant missionary would push hard all morning, eat short lunches, tract all afternoon, eat a quick dinner, and then stay out all evening working. I scheduled one too many appointments all the time. With all the miles we walked and lunches we skipped, I sometimes caught colds. And the sniffles and sore throats and exhaustion didn't seem to go away. I was perpetually sick. I thought maybe I wasn't a good missionary. I remember leaning against the hot water pipes on the wall next to the toilet, feeling grateful that I could finally rest, and dreaming of going home.

Then one day as I was praying, the Holy Ghost touched my mind. *Sister Lammers, the adversary is trying to get you. He knows he can't take you down with some more obvious sin, so instead he's tricking you into burning out. He is getting at you through your pride. You are running faster than you have strength because you want to prove you are awesome. By making yourself sick, you aren't disrupting Satan's kingdom, and you aren't helping the Lord's kingdom anymore. With you sick in bed, he wins.*

Wow. Satan is sneaky. I had contracted a case of "Don't Take Care of Yourself-itis." Thank the Lord for this loving course correction! He was merciful enough to show me what a poor path I had chosen. I started eating better and more often, exercising regularly, and getting more sleep. Months of mystery illness disappeared.

These steps of physical health are rooted in the plan of salvation. We believe that in this life we can begin, through Christ, to refine our spirits and become more like him. We're not waiting for the next life to get a jump on our spiritual salvation. Our physical salvation is no different. We should not wait for the Resurrection to pursue whatever level of health is available to us! *There are major blessings available to sisters who follow the Word of Wisdom.* When we properly care for our bodies, we will feel a greater measure of the Holy Ghost with us. We will be able to better discern the still, small voice, and we'll have more energy and enthusiasm to carry out His will for us and for others.

You cannot separate your body and your spirit. You wouldn't want to! Doctrine and Covenants 88:15 teaches, "The spirit and the body are the soul of man." You need your body to experience a fulness of joy! Furthermore, this principle will help you better understand ordinances because the Lord cares about the whole soul—your body *and* your spirit. In nourishing your body, you are nourishing your spirit. Only then will you have the strength to nourish others.

Mission Health Tips from Dawn Wessman, Personal Trainer

1. Sleep seven to nine hours at night. If sleeping is difficult for you, examine your level of physical fitness. Daily exercise makes for deeper sleep. Talk to a doctor if you are having sleeping difficulties. Sleep deprivation causes memory loss, irritability, and a lowered immune system.

2. Walk. Sometimes we assume walking is wimpy, but it is not! Briskly walking a mile and jogging a mile burn the same amount of calories. Walk with others in well-lit places. If the local women don't go there, neither should you. Remember always to wear good shoes.

3. Learn how to do indoor exercises. Sometimes you need to work out inside for weather or safety reasons. Moderate

weight-lifting, door exercises, Pilates, yoga, jump-roping, and abdominal exercises will help you stay fit and well.

4. Find a regular time to exercise. And when you do, exercise with your companion—it will add a fun dimension to your relationship. Working out releases chemicals through your body that give you feelings of hope and optimism.

5. Find good recipes with greens, beans, and lean proteins. It may be tempting to grab sugar cereal and boxed meals, but learning to cook a few healthy go-to meals will bless you physically on the mission. Many healthy soups, chilies, and salads will last you throughout the week when made ahead of time.

6. Drink plenty of water. Counting the number of glasses a day is nearly impossible, so instead, trust your urine. (Yes, I just said that word, Sister.) Your urine should be the color of light lemonade. Don't go for the gold. The more hydrated you are, the better your body can use food to create energy. You will be sluggish without enough water.

DAWN WESSMAN is a mother, BYU-grad, certified personal trainer and group exercise instructor in Boston. She stars in the workout video "Wedding Body Pilates," and develops online fitness programs for mothers. She also writes for the Power of Moms website, where she manages the "Bloom" self-improvement game. She continues learning from, laughing with, and trying out new mom tricks on her five small children. She can do more push-ups than you.

Photo by Marilyn Linge

My Carnegie Hall
Lisa Stratton Sorenson

Carnegie Hall. The majestic New York City venue entices most musicians as an Olympic stadium would a runner. When I started playing piano at the age of five and violin at ten, I hardly had my sights set on a Carnegie Hall performance, but as my musical life continued, the allure of such a place became real. To me, it represented an ultimate conquest in the world of musical talent.

Thanks to a few lucky opportunities in high school and countless of hours of practicing, Carnegie Hall became more palpable to me. When I was only a freshman, my high school symphony was invited to perform at the Youth & Music Festival in Vienna, Austria. To earn money for the trip, we hired ourselves out in small chamber groups. For these gigs, we memorized our music and walked around dining areas, dodging tuxedoed waiters carrying trays of hors d'oeurves. I performed for politicians, movie stars, and even British royalty. After one performance, I met Prince Charles! He was my father's height and admired my friend's cello. Another time, I played background music while Loren Green (from the TV series *Bonanza*) ate a steak. In '80s teen-speak it was, "like, totally awesome." Once in Austria, our symphony played in magnificent cathedrals, tall and ornate with exquisite stained glass windows. A year later, in another city youth orchestra, I travelled to Mexico and performed in beautiful plazas around Chihuahua and Juarez. By the time I graduated from high school, my violin and I had ventured halfway around the world. Eager to set aside the hideous maroon polyester orchestra uniform I had been wearing, I left home for more sophisticated orchestral adventures in college.

When I arrived at BYU, I auditioned my way into the BYU Philharmonic. Once again, the opportunities seemed endless. Playing in pit orchestras allowed me front-row seats to wondrous operas and musicals. I participated in the BYU Homecoming Spectacular and performed in the Tabernacle on Temple Square in Salt Lake City. I played once again for state dignitaries and entertainers, as well as numerous LDS church leaders. During my junior year, I made it into the most competitive string group in the university: the BYU Chamber Orchestra. I remember fondly playing Prokofiev's "Peter and the Wolf" as Elder Holland (the president of BYU at the time) and Sister Holland read the story. A year later, even though I hadn't majored in music, I prepared a senior recital. I practiced for hours a day, and in the spring of my senior year, performed a solo program entitled "Cat Gut, Horse Hair, and Tree Limbs: A Musical Dissection," giving a nod to my actual studies in the premed track of zoology. A virtuoso I was not, but in the musical world I could walk the walk.

As time progressed, I realized I wanted to serve a mission, but the thought of closing my violin case and not practicing, performing, or feeling the camaraderie of a musical group for eighteen months was unimaginable. I had grown accustomed to this association multiple times a week for over a decade. I was hesitant. But I learned that the Chamber Orchestra would tour Europe the semester I returned, so with that to look forward to, I decided to make the sacrifice. I resolved wholeheartedly to set my violin aside and serve the Lord.

I was called to the Alabama Birmingham Mission, where most people worried about things other than which type of rosin to buy for a violin bow. There I met a sister who had fled political persecution in Uganda. She introduced me to chocolate-covered grasshoppers. I became friends with a woman from Puerto Rico who offered to spend the only dollar in her purse to buy a cake mix in order to bring refreshments for a fireside. I watched happy children with cornrowed hair spending their summer free time doing flips on old, insect-infested mattresses piled in a vacant lot. I could feel the Spirit pouring from them. They were wonderful.

I walked, tracted, and sweated through a long, hot summer in Alabama. When we entered people's homes, my companion and I would discreetly race inside, hoping to sit by a fan, or maybe even a window unit air conditioner! We tucked our skirts close to our thighs while seated on tattered couches so cockroaches wouldn't crawl up our legs. We had to field proposals from creepy men asking us to have their babies. And within the ward I attended, it was no surprise that my piano-playing ability immediately came into high demand. Where I served, no one had the opportunity to be musically trained. More than one of the branches I served in met in rented space, with a haphazard collection of tables, chairs, and hymnals, where the only "piano" to speak of was an electric keyboard. These arrangements led me to wonder whether synthetic music could uplift anyone. Would the members actually feel the Spirit while I played a sacred hymn about the Atonement if I accidentally hit the disco beat button?

As the months progressed, I played more and more. My perspective on my talents began to shift. When Elder Hartman Rector Jr. came to tour our mission, he asked that a missionary accompany him on the piano as he sang. I was asked just a day ahead of time to be that accompanist, and was, of course, nervous.

I had never played the song before. During the meeting, I said a silent prayer asking for help, and I truly felt the Holy Ghost sustaining me through the song. For the first time I saw my talents used for a higher purpose than just the cultural benefit of those listening. On another occasion, someone borrowed a violin for me to play at the summer mission party. The violin was a beat-up student violin that wasn't even my size, and I could hardly play the thing. It was as if I were starving and someone handed me moldy bread. To make matters worse, the morning of the party, we were playing games and I broke my finger! What a sight I was, trying to play a junky violin, without the use of all ten fingers! I was depressed. But as the following weeks progressed, I kept playing the piano for meetings. I learned to play a decent nine-finger version of "O Divine Redeemer" by stretching my splinted finger up out of the way. The idea of playing the violin and piano for purposes other than my own self-gratification was germinating.

It wasn't until I reached my fourth area, North Birmingham, that my understanding of my musical talents fundamentally changed. The area covered yet another humble branch meeting in a rented space, home to dear members, some of whom thought nothing of shouting "Praise the Lord" during a prayer. One Sunday, a woman read most of her talk from a Billy Graham magazine, followed by a visiting high councilor who paced during his address, raising his voice like a televangelist. As was common throughout Alabama, we missionaries were the only white-skinned people in the congregation. During sacrament meeting, the children would sandwich their little hands around mine and say it looked "like an Oreo" two chocolate layers stuffed with white cream filling. We'd reverently giggle during sacrament meeting.

I was again playing an electric keyboard for sacrament meeting, Relief Society, and occasionally Primary. After a few weeks, the branch president heard that I played the violin too and asked if I would play at a fireside. Because of my experience trying to play a violin at the mission party the year before, I dreaded it but knew I couldn't decline the request. Through some convoluted connection, just a day or two before the fireside, a violin was placed in my hands. Once again this "violin" could only be called a violin because it was shaped as such and had four strings. It was another piece of junk that sounded as if it hadn't been tuned since Bach wrote his first sonata. The collegiate pseudo-professional in me kicked in again, and I smirked at the thought of trying to eke music out of this piece of wood. I didn't want to perform. I would sound terrible all over again! I didn't have any music besides the hymn book, which I felt couldn't adequately represent what I had to offer. By the time we were on our way to the fireside, I still hadn't decided what to play.

There were about twenty people at the fireside seated on the church-issue hard, metal folding chairs. The elders started things off by showing part of the video *How Rare a Possession*. This church production had been released a couple months previously and we regularly showed it to investigators using a portable VCR that we'd lug from house to house. My turn came too quickly after the movie and I had no choice but to step up to the front. I decided to start with "Our Savior's Love" since it was the background music we had just heard in the video. I then talked a bit about the early Latter-day Saints, muddled through a hesitant verse of "Come, Come, Ye Saints," and then began my testimony of Joseph Smith—how he had sacrificed so much, just like the Saints in *How Rare a Possession*. I explained that in the Carthage Jail, Joseph asked John Taylor to sing the hymn "A Poor Wayfaring Man." At this point a wave of emotion hit me and I had to stop talking and just breathe, trying to regain my composure. After a moment, I raised my violin, placed the bow on the strings, and began to play the hymn. I was no longer a musically rusty missionary trying to coax a melody out of a subpar instrument. My fingers felt literally guided. The only sound in the room was the poignant melody I produced. The collection of faces in the congregation gazed at me with pure love for my song. The Spirit was tangible. I later wrote in my journal that it was the best "performance" I'd ever given.

Something changed in me that day, something that I didn't realize needed changing. Clearly up until then, I had viewed my talents as something for me to pursue, a vehicle for me to achieve personal success and make conquests. In reality, the optimal use of my talents right then and there, in a rented store front, was to share the message of the Savior with a simple, unaccompanied song. Nothing fancy, no practicing needed, just music from my heart and soul. In the weeks that followed, my piano accompaniments took on a more sacred meaning for me. My motions were no longer mechanical, moving fingers and playing notes. I was worshipping my Savior.

Three months later, my eighteen months of missionary service concluded. I considered staying home for a couple months to earn some money for college, but my violin and the long-anticipated BYU Chamber Orchestra European trip called to me. I was eager to return to college. Unfortunately life intervened and my plans changed. I was only home for a week, but it was long enough for me to suffer whiplash in a mild car accident and return to BYU in a neck brace—not the fashion accessory of my choice. (After all, with my newly permed hair I was hoping to be a hip RM.) Regrettably the accident had a bigger impact than I initially realized. Because I was in a neck brace, I couldn't even hold my violin to practice. My placement audition during the first week of school was horrible, and I was not readmitted into the Chamber Orchestra. I would not be going on the European tour. I probably could have pled my case to the conductor—after all, I had to wear the neck brace for only a couple more weeks, but it was okay. I was okay. My perspective on my talents had changed and I didn't need another trip to Austria, with its stained glass windows, apple strudel, and beaming audiences, to give me another notch in my performance belt. I understood God's plan for my abilities on a deeper level. He didn't give me this gift just to let me dazzle people in fancy venues, however much I enjoyed that. He gave me this gift so that I could use it to serve.

I still think about my "best performance" as a missionary from time to time, especially when I dust off my violin case to play for a baptism, our stake's annual *Messiah* sing-along, or for a special musical number in sacrament meeting. More often, my musical offerings are even less grandiose. Three times I have squeezed into my old prom dress, donned a pink, pointed princess hat, and played the role of Royal Musician at my three daughters' kindergarten Medieval fairs. This is the version of royalty for which I now perform.

I'm definitely rusty now that all the musically distracting years have taken their toll, but I recently had another "best" performance. This one took place in a nursing home where I serenaded a ninety-year-old widow with songs and hymns of her request. I played alone for her in a small, fluorescently lit room with wilting flowers at the bedside table. Even though I had visited her with my violin a few times over the years, this was a sacred half hour—one last opportunity to lift her soul with music before she died a couple weeks later. Once again my fingers were guided and heaven was near. This is what the Lord intended for my talents. These unassuming performances have become my Carnegie Hall.

LISA STRATTON SORENSON graduated from BYU in zoology premed, followed by Northeastern University's program in health information administration. She lives in the Boston area with her husband and their four children. In addition to motherly duties, she works part-time as a clinical data specialist. She loved her mission in Alabama and still involuntarily says "y'all" from time to time.

"Angels Round About"
Jennifer Rockwood Knight

ant, pant, pant, burn. I. Will. Never. Adjust. To. These. Hills. I had to will my legs to keep pumping the bike onward toward our next appointment. Even though I had already been in Taiwan for over a year, my quads never seemed to master the steep mountainous climbs in Muzha, my quaintly rural area bordering Taipei City. I certainly never stopped panting. My hair never seemed to stop molding, either. The humidity relentlessly prevented my ponytailed-hair from drying in the twenty-three hours after I showered before I tried to wash it clean again.

My junior companion led us up the mountain, both of us struggling to ride faster so we would make our appointment in time. Suddenly, I felt as if someone were standing behind my shoulder. We were biking so slowly, someone easily could have been following on foot, so I glanced back to see who it was. Only the public bus disappeared down the hill. *I wish that were me,* I thought as a drop of sweat trickled down my neck. Almost immediately, I felt something strangely tangible, yet completely invisible, tug my attention toward my left-hand side. Quickly scanning the scene, I saw a small woman seated on a bus bench, waiting for the next bus. *Yep. One of the millions of people we could contact on this tiny island. We are going to be late!* I stood up and pushed hard on my pedals to speed up my bike, but the nagging feeling only heightened. I looked again. This time I noticed that woman's hunched shoulders and blank stare.

Sigh. I guess we could take a few minutes to contact her. But there was no way I could get my companion's attention. She was too far ahead. At that moment, she glanced over at the woman and then quickly stopped her own bike. She looked back at me, and without any words, we both headed across the street to contact her.

The woman seemed lost in a trance, quietly pondering something significant. Even after we stood in front of her, her empty eyes barely registered our presence. She did not seem to wonder who we were or why we were standing so close to her. I felt the unseen nudge again.

"Hello, miss. We are representatives of Jesus Christ," I said. "We have a message to share with you about families. We want to talk to you about how families can be together forever, even after death."

At this, her empty eyes filled with emotion, immediately spilling tears down her face. "Even after death?" She began crying harder. My companion and I flanked her tiny frame, embracing her from each side. We held her as her body went limp with sobs.

Not quite a month before, her twenty-one-year-old son had died. He had been walking to class when a car hit and killed him. This dear woman, our quickly-beloved Wang Wei, felt smothered beneath this burden. It was too much to bear in a life already full of pain and heartache. Only a year before her son's death, her husband had left her for a mistress and family he had started on a business trip to mainland China. After his son's death, he returned but only to claim some of the insurance money. Wang Wei's other son struggled to find an identity and had started experimenting with all kinds of things—things that made Wang Wei's heart hurt even more.

This first meeting at the bus stop, she later told us, had been timely. She had hit rock bottom and was wallowing in despair. We had come at just the right moment to save her from herself. This first discussion seemed to resuscitate her, and we noticed her eyes begin to fill with light again. She readily agreed to come to church.

She showed up to sacrament meeting in jeans and a sweatshirt and tucked herself between me and my companion, linking her arms through ours. She absorbed everything like a sponge. In Sunday School, the teacher began talking about temples. Wei did not know what a temple was, nor did she know what went on inside of one. We had only taught her the first discussion about God our Father. Still, I could see her listening intently as we spoke of this connection between the dead and the living.

This topic hit close to my heart too. I had also lost a loved one just weeks before, about the same time Wei's son died. I remember answering the phone in Chinese and hearing my father's voice. My heart stopped. My dad, fighting to hold in his own emotion, told me my dear Grandma Alyce ("Grandma Al") had suffered a debilitating stroke and passed away that morning. I sat listening to the details of her passing, feeling numb. She wasn't that old. This wasn't supposed to happen.

In the days after her passing, I was a wreck. Here I was, a missionary, supposed to be teaching others about joy and happiness, but I would frequently fall into tears in the middle of a discussion without warning. I could not seem to shake my disappointment that I would never get to see or hug her again. She was gone.

One morning I opened my scriptures to Mosiah 16. My mind saw an Arnold Friberg Abinadi teaching the wicked King Noah (leopards crouched menacingly at his feet, of course.) I read and heard his words in a rush of the Spirit, "But there is a resurrection, therefore the grave hath no victory, and the sting of death is swallowed up in Christ." I felt encircled by love—love that felt so real and whole and personal, I almost believed it was a person. It felt like a loving grandmother embracing her grieving granddaughter, giving her one last hug. Just like that, the sting of her death softened.

Perhaps because of this experience, as we sat in the temple lesson that morning, I felt the familiar tears wet my cheeks again. I still felt terribly raw, and though my own pain lessened every day, it empathetically connected me to Wang Wei. I testified to the class that I knew I would see my grandmother again because of the sealing power Christ gave us through the temple. After the lesson, Wang Wei's eyes bored into mine. "I want to go to that place!" she exclaimed. "I want to help my son . . . and your grandma."

★ ★ ★ ★ ★

At the second appointment, she ushered us into her damp apartment and gave us warm cups of water, even though the temperature and humidity screamed for a cooler beverage. We sat on the couch and asked her how she felt. "*Hai keyi*," she replied. Just all right. I thought, *that's to be expected*. The mist creeping down the lush green mountains made the entire room dark, so Wang Wei gently brushed her finger across the bottom of her touch-sensitive lamp, and it flickered on. We could better see the expression on her face. She looked . . . hopeful?

My companion opened the flip chart and asked to say a prayer. Wang Wei curled her petite legs under her. Her face, clean without makeup, bowed a little, and we prayed. The mist suddenly felt really thick, as if it had spilled over the mountains and crept into the apartment; but instead of feeling cold or dark, it enveloped us in warmth. I remembered this fulness from my grandmother's passing: a love personified.

My companion, Sister Beus, talked about temples and covenants, about life after death, and about Christ making it possible for us to live again. She then flipped to the page on the chart with all the commitments we make before going through the temple and paused. In a split second, Wang Wei turned to Sister Beus. "Yes," she switched her eyes to mine. "I'm willing. I'm willing to do it all. I just want to be with my son."

The light flickered off and then back on. Wang Wei casually remarked, "He's here, you know. My son is here. That's why the lights flashed. But I'm not scared." Normally, a statement like this would have elicited a raised-eyebrow exchange with my companion. I might have put it in my "Yeah Right" Hall of Fame along with the woman who claimed Jesus came to nurse from her at night or the investigator who claimed she was the prophet, not President Hinckley.

My companion and I looked at each other. We both felt it. He *was* there.

It didn't even feel strange or out of place. On a mission, this kind of stuff happened all the time, though it never ceased to make me marvel. I reflected on the scripture I had chosen for my mission plaque, "And whoso receiveth you, there will I be also, for I will go before your face. I will be on your right hand and on your left, and my Spirit shall be in your hearts, and mine angels round about you to bear you up" (D&C 84:88). These feelings—these angels—were not just normal, they were expected on a mission.

Memories flashed through my subconscious: the discussion I distinctly felt as if unnamed ancestors sat close to our investigator as we taught, waiting and hoping; the time we felt prompted to shop at a different market on preparation day, miraculously running into that less-active member we could never reach at home; that night we rode home followed by a cat-eyed man with a devilish grin who rode within striking distance of my bike but then abruptly stopped, somehow unable to follow anymore. I remember the thought that immediately followed, "Fear not, there are legions of angels protecting you." When all these things happened, I recognized the miracle, but I was not surprised. Of course that happened on a mission. The Lord said it would.

This is why it felt so natural to find a mini miracle all set up awaiting our arrival at Wang Wei's house the next time we dropped in on her. For weeks, she had been trying to persuade her other (wayward) son and her dead son's girlfriend to listen to our message. All these new truths resounded so strongly with her; she felt more hope than she had felt in a long time. She wanted her family to feel that peace too, and she had nearly convinced them. But skeptical that it was really as good as she professed, they were reluctant to meet with the missionaries. In a funny coincidence, Wei's son ran into the elders while at the market a few days prior and agreed to let them come to his house. He lost his nerve shortly thereafter and ditched the appointment to go to Wang Wei's house with his brother's girlfriend. We must have been God's plan B because we rang Wei's doorbell precisely at the time the elders were probably ringing his empty apartment doorbell a town away.

Wang Wei beamed as she opened the door. "Oh, how funny! Here they are right now! Guys, *these* are the missionaries I've been telling you about. Come in, sisters!" Shock with a hint of fear laced their stilted conversation with us. They agreed to listen to what we had to say. We began the discussion. I could see the same emptiness in their eyes that I'd seen in Wang Wei's just a few weeks before. I felt compelled to talk about temples and the eternal life of families. Sister Beus tag-teamed into how Christ made it all possible. Wei's son listened intently. He put down his cigarette and leaned forward. The girlfriend pulled her knee up on her chair and hugged it as she asked question after question. I remember most feeling like there were more than five of us around the table.

I finally asked, "Will you come to church this Sunday?" Like a breath pulled in straining to exhale, we waited; those unseen waited. The room, crowded with anticipation, sat still and damp. Then . . . Wei's son picked up his cigarette again and leaned back in his chair. The girlfriend put her knee down, adjusted her weight, and broke eye contact. "*Yuanfen de hua,*" the son said between draws on his cigarette. If fate arranges it. *Hmmm* . . . I had been in Taiwan long enough to know when the Chinese started talking about *yuanfen* (fate), it was a respectful way to tell us our message was not part of their fate. They were brushing us off.

Sister Beus pulled a Book of Mormon out of her bag anyway, bore testimony, and gave it to them. We still gave them details about our Sunday meetings, but I sensed from their vigorous head nodding that the words rolled off their ears to the ground unheard. We said our good-byes and shuffled out, Wei disappointedly shutting the door behind us. As we left, the words came to mind, "I will go before your face. . . . And my Spirit shall be in your hearts, and mine angels round about you" (D&C 84:88). I felt reassured that we had played our role exactly as God had intended, despite the outcome.

We knew this encounter would be hard on Wei; she longed for the support of her last remaining family members. Still, we felt confident she would stay strong in her commitment to the gospel truths she had so readily accepted. When we arrived for her next appointment, she wasn't there. She stopped answering or returning our phone calls. She didn't come to church.

We kept working, praying, and fasting for Wei. We knew our limits, but we stretched ourselves to find how deep our faith could go. We believed what Moroni said: "it is by faith that miracles are wrought; and it is by faith that angels . . . minister unto men" and "by the ministering of angels . . . men began to exercise faith in Christ" (Moroni 7:37, 25). We knew that if we did our part, the angels would do their part. We had witnessed as much already. And so we waited.

One night, as we made our nightly phone calls to investigators and appointments we had the next day, we dialed Wang Wei with a prepared voice message to leave on her phone. Instead, we heard the phone click. "Hello?" she said. Shocked, Sister Beus enthusiastically greeted her, and they began chatting and laughing like old friends. Her family was not ready to accept the gospel, she said. They thought she was crazy, that this was an American church and besides, she could never live the way we asked her to live. She said she had really considered their opinion and realized they were right. She did not want to lose her Chinese identity or pressure herself to live up to such a high standard. But the more she tried to convince herself that the Church was not a good fit for her, the more she just wanted that feeling back. She wanted to feel close to her son again. The room felt crowded once more as we set up another time to meet. This time, I also felt a familiar grandmotherly warmth around me again. So many unseen helpers, so much invisible joy.

★ ★ ★ ★ ★

Our hearts nearly burst as we watched Wei, dressed in white, step down into the font. It was not the first time I'd seen a soul come to baptism, nor would it be the last, but this time, heaven felt incredibly close. We were surrounded by love and joy, encompassed with peace. We watched Wei's once-empty eyes pop open as she came out of the water. They were full of light now. Later, the elder confirming her a member of the Church commanded, "Receive the Holy Ghost" and I felt a rush, as if thousands of people unseen hurried to her side. We knew her son was there. We saw confirmation in the tears of joy that wet her face—nothing like those bus stop tears we had witnessed only a few weeks before. I heard in my head again the words of my mission scripture, "And whoso receiveth you, there will I be also." Now I remembered that feeling—a trace of what it must have felt like to stand in God's presence. This was why I came on a mission. As my companion and I rode our bikes home that night, we both felt a little lighter . . . almost as if we rode with angels.

JENNIFER ROCKWOOD KNIGHT thrives on action, whether it's raising her four children, writing, running, teaching, or traveling abroad. She recently finished a thesis examining declining church attendance among Christian singles in the United States, which culminated in a master's in liberal arts in extension studies from Harvard University. After that arduous pursuit, her husband, Kurt, now tries to encourage more relaxing activities like knitting and sleeping. It doesn't work.

My Heart is Locked . . . I Think

Anonymous

t was my first time walking into the mission home.

I am totally ready for this . . . all those hours in the MTC running stairs while memorizing irregular verb conjugations . . . all the early mornings studying scriptures with a flashlight before my roommates woke up . . . all those times I felt the Holy Ghost as I taught, even though it was just a fake investigator in the Teaching Resource Center . . . now it is really starting! Awesome. I followed the other missionaries into the spacious living room and squeezed together with the sisters on the paisley sofa, trying to contain my enthusiasm.

"Welcome, elders and sisters," said the middle-aged man standing in the center of the room. "As you've probably figured out, I am your mission president, this is my wife, and these are my assistants, Elder Thompson and Elder Ferreira.[10] I need to interview each of you, and we'll start with the sisters. While I am conducting these interviews for the next few hours, please study the scriptures or write in your journals, and enjoy our fresh *cajú* and *acerola* juices."

President's voice trailed off. *What a fabulous house. Wow, his wife is more beautiful in real life than in the* Church News *picture. And there are the assistants, one Brazilian and one . . . American.* My gaze rested on Elder Thompson. *Is it just me or does he smile like Harrison Ford?*

---

10 Names have been changed.

What a very good-looking eld—Oh, darn it; I'm a missionary now. I glanced down at my name tag to remind myself of my calling.

"Sister Gates—"

"Yes," I said, snapping back to reality.

"I said you're first, Sister Gates," President said. "Please follow me. No time to lose."

★ ★ ★ ★ ★

After the interview, I stared at the pages of my Book of Mormon for a while before I gave up. I had already studied for an hour that morning at the MTC, three hours at the airport, and the whole plane ride. I was too excited to finally be there. Besides, after two months cooped up in MTC classrooms, Sister Green and I couldn't help but gaze longingly at the dining room's gracious, open double doors that beckoned us outside. We decided to take a break to try the juice and scope out the yard.

Outside, the *pings* and *whacks* coming from the side of the house immediately caught our attention. We followed our ears to a heated ping-pong match out on the porch. *So this is where the assistants went.* I smiled as they greeted us, and then Sister Green and I started practicing Portuguese with the mission president's teenage daughter, who was doing her English homework on the porch. I tried to focus on the daughter, but sitting in front of a good game got my competitive juices flowing, and I couldn't help but watch. *That American is pretty good.* When Elder Ferreira finally lost the game and moved to place the paddle in the basket under the table (saying something about the Anti-Nephi-Lehis burying their weapons of war), I jumped up and grabbed the paddle from him.

"My turn!" My face turned red as I realized those words had come from my mouth. *Whoops. Where was that quiet dignity? Wait—am I even allowed to play ping-pong with an elder?* I hesitated, trying to remember if there was a missionary rule prohibiting coed ping-pong.

"All right, bring it on, Sister Gates," Elder Thompson challenged, reading my name tag. *It must be okay.*

Just watch the ball, I coached myself. He served; I won the first point. And the next few. I started feeling pretty good. But then I looked up and our eyes met as I started my serve. My hands started sweating. *Stop. You've played against lots of good-looking guys—and you don't even know this one. You're not trying to impress him—you're only trying to beat him!* I overshot the table and then lost the next several points. Elder Thompson started making small talk in English, asking about my family, why I'd come on a mission, and how the food in the MTC had been. We'd all made a pact with an MTC teacher to speak Portuguese every moment in the mission field, so I held on to the ball for a minute to concentrate on my responses. He laughed.

"You're American, aren't you?" he asked, pointedly raising one eyebrow.

"*Sim.*"

"So am I. You can speak English with me." He motioned for me to serve.

"*Obrigada*—but I prefer Portuguese." C'mon, stay cool. *Concentrate on the game.*

"Okay, whatever," he responded, sharing a look with Elder Ferreira that said, "Let's humor the greenies." Little by little, I caught up to tie the game at 17. Just then, the other American sisters, my MTC roommates, walked out to see what all the noise was about. They dragged the scattered patio chairs together and started watching the game. *I can do this.* I took the lead, 18–17, then 19–17, then 20–17, 20–18, 20–19. *Don't choke.* 21–19. Game. *I WON! Win with quiet dignity, Caroline—I mean Sister Gates. Just a small smile.*

"Good game, Sister Gates," Elder Thompson conceded, ignoring his companion's taunts about being dethroned as the mission champion. He walked around the table to shake my hand.

"You too," I said as his firm grip closed around my hand. I looked up to meet his gaze, and he winked at me. At least, I thought he did. It was hard to tell—maybe he had a gnat near his eye? My cheeks grew hot. "Well, I . . . um . . . I need to go study my grammar now," I stammered and walked back inside.

With my adrenaline still coursing and my emotions scrambled, I stared at the black squiggles on the pages and tried to remember that missionary talk we'd read by President Kimball, the one that decreed, "thou shalt not flirt" and "lock your heart and leave the key at home."[11]

★ ★ ★ ★ ★

"Did you notice Elder Thompson?" an MTC roommate, Sister Green, remarked that evening as we brushed our teeth with bottled water. Funny she should ask. I'd just finished praying for forgiveness for the afternoon's momentary distraction from missionary work. This was not the conversation I wanted to have.

"I saw the way he was looking at you, Sister Gates. You'd better watch out, at least for the next sixteen months," Sister Green teased.

"Oh no, I didn't notice anything. Which one was he—the Brazilian or the American assistant?" I feigned ignorance, hoping they would buy it.

"You shook his hand after ping-pong," the roommate protested knowingly.

"Well, anyway, my heart is locked," I declared before I spit out my toothpaste. "And that's the end of it."

11 Spencer W. Kimball, "Lock Your Heart." Latin American Mission Tour, 1968. At missionaryhelper.com/talks/lockheart.html.

★ ★ ★ ★ ★

After several months of missionary sweat, tears, and joy in a zone far away from the mission office, I was transferred back to the main city. I felt like Country Mouse when I walked into the full chapel for my first mission conference. I had no idea there were so many missionaries in our mission, and it was powerful realizing we were all there to build Zion. I scanned the sea of anonymous white shirts looking for MTC classmates, but instead I found *him*. *How does he stick out in the crowd like that? Is it just a righteous glow?*

I took my assigned seat at the piano and started to play some prelude music. A visiting member of the Seventy gave an inspiring talk about serving with *all* your heart, might, mind and strength. His talk was spiritually and intellectually riveting, and I couldn't take notes fast enough. It was just as fabulous as general conference!

As I played one of my favorites hymns for postlude, Elder Thompson moseyed over to the piano, coiling a microphone cord.

"Thanks for playing today, Sister Gates," he said.

"Sure—it's no big deal." I smiled, continuing to play.

"This is my favorite hymn," he said, almost too quietly to hear.

"Oh, cool." And then he moved on to organize the clean-up effort. I tucked my hair behind my ear and straightened up on the piano bench with that proud, schoolgirlish thrill of being noticed by the popular boy. But then I started to laugh at myself. *Don't even give a second thought to what just happened. He was in charge of the meeting, and he just thanked you for helping.*

President had instructed those who wanted quick interviews to line up with their companions outside the CES office, the only air-conditioned room in the building. My senior companion jumped at the chance. We sat in line in the breezeway, hoping to catch some gusts of wind during the sweaty hours chatting and waiting. President finally invited my companion in. I said good-bye to the two departing elders but then heard voices coming from the chapel. *Funny—I thought everyone had gone.* I tiptoed over to the chapel and saw the last two elders shaking hands with Elder Thompson before they walked out the door. I noiselessly scampered back to my bag. *This isn't good. But if he stays in the chapel and I stay here, it'll be fine. Let's see—study scriptures or write a letter?* I whipped out a piece of paper and began to recount the week's happenings to my parents. After a minute, I heard the noisy chapel ceiling fans slowing to a stop and the chapel door squeaking and thumping closed. Then I heard footsteps growing louder. *Uh oh.*

"Hi, Elder Thompson, you're still here?" I asked.

"Yeah, I'm just waiting for Pres. We have some stuff to do when he finishes. My comp. went with the other office elders. Is Pres. in there with your companion?"

"Yes, they just started."

"Oh boy, we're in for a wait. She really likes to talk," he sighed.

"You're right about that," I laughed. I couldn't figure out why my voice sounded strange until I realized that I was speaking in English. Oops. I started to feel a little uncomfortable. *Never be alone with anyone of the opposite sex. Good thing I memorized that rule book. But what can I do about it?!*

He leaned against the church's iron security gate opposite me, folding his arms casually, and resting one foot on a lower bar, settling in for a wait. I nervously turned back to my letter. But he kept talking to me. "You've been doing good work, Sister Gates. That was pretty amazing how quickly you memorized all the lessons."

"Thanks." *Me? Good work? Flattering—actually, great! I don't think I'm that good, but I sure am trying hard. But how does he even know? And why isn't he leaving? Maybe this is an interview?*

"I saw you guys baptized someone this past weekend," he said.

"Oh, Fernanda's baptism was beautiful. She was our second baptism. A young man in the ward baptized her, and he loved it so much that he's begging us to teach all his friends so he can baptize them! We're also working with a wonderful family now—José and Maria and their three teenagers." We talked about their situation for a couple of minutes before the conversation lulled.

"So, Gates, where'd you learn to play ping-pong like that? There aren't many girls that good."

Girls? I think he just called me a girl. Okay, first of all, I am a woman, and second, he should call me Sister Gates. Ughh . . . sometimes these elders are so clueless. I tried quelling my fluttering heart with righteous indignation, but it didn't help—his twinkling blue eyes were very compelling.

"Oh, I played club table tennis in college. Slamming the ball was a good way to relieve stress—as long as someone else paid to replace all the deformed ping-pong balls." We both chuckled. As the conversation moved back to missionary work and spiritual principles, I felt myself slowly relaxing. It was fun to talk with this smart, handsome guy, even if he was younger than me. The discussion flowed so naturally. I felt much more comfortable talking with him than with any of my companions, and speaking English made me feel like myself again. His wise, seasoned counsel on missionary work was inspiring, and I was excited to implement some of his ideas. *He is just the kind of man I'd like to marry. Wait. Delete that thought!* A while later, the doorknob squeaked and I suddenly remembered how scandalous this unintended encounter might appear. I grabbed my bag, stood up, smiled at Sister da Silva, shook hands with President and Elder Thompson, and hustled away with Sister da Silva to catch the bus, still beaming.

★ ★ ★ ★ ★

On preparation day a week later, the mission president's Chevrolet Blazer showed up in front of our apartment. I went downstairs to see why President had come and to open the pad-locked outer gate for him while Sister da Silva frantically washed the dishes. It was actually Elders Thompson and Ferreira. I talked through the SUV window with Elder Ferreira, who said they were going to move two more sisters into our apartment that week, and we needed to get our place ready for them. I looked at Elder Harrison Ford in the driver's seat. *He looks really great in a baseball hat.* "Yankees, Elder Thompson? Really?" I smirked. He nodded toward my Dodgers shirt and taunted, "C'mon Gates, anyone who likes the Dodgers shouldn't talk smack." I had a hard time containing my smile as I waved while they drove off. It was fun having a good-looking friend in a high place.

To stop mentally replaying that borderline flirtatious encoun-ter, I started to memorize hymns in Portuguese—and it worked! I carried my little hymnal everywhere I went. It's hard to think of anything else when the brain is running "Scatter Sunshine" on repeat. *Luz espalhai em todo o seu caminho. . . .*

★ ★ ★ ★ ★

A mission choir tour of shopping centers provided the oppor-tunity for our friendship to progress. Because there was no telling when a bus would come or how bad traffic would be, we all tried to arrive well before performance time. After my companion and I tried contacting the shoppers and bored mall employees, we'd socialize with missionaries we rarely saw outside of choir. Instead of just once a transfer, I started to see Elder Thompson a couple times each week. Sometimes he would just nod and raise his eye-brows at me across the room as we made eye contact, and other times we chatted for thirty seconds or so with tons of missionar-ies all around us—usually with one or both of our companions.

Though I knew the rule—"Refer to other missionaries . . . as 'Elder' or 'Sister' and their surnames, not by . . . surnames alone," I started to drop the "Elder" when talking with him. I was a little chagrined that I could break a rule so easily, but everyone did it and it didn't seem that big an indiscretion. Nothing else was untoward—talking with everyone was part of his assignment—and for him, I was just part of "everyone." But I couldn't help but feel he paid special attention to me. Or maybe I just wanted him to pay special attention to me?

As the weeks wore on, I found myself looking forward to choir for the wrong reasons. I prayed for help to stop thinking about him. I tried to ignore him and went out of my way to avoid him, but somehow I could always spot him out of the corner of my eye. Each time I saw him, it would take me progressively longer to refocus on missionary work and to hear the still, small voice guiding me.

★ ★ ★ ★ ★

The refiner's fire heated up quickly when the assistants came to our zone meeting one Tuesday with the message that I'd be training in a new area. Elder Thompson explained that I needed to find an apartment before the missionaries from the MTC arrived the following week, and he'd be my office liaison to help me with the details. Instead of returning to our area to teach, I found myself pouring over a map with Elder Harrison Ford, working to figure out the optimal housing location relative to the various bus routes and the area's exact geographic center. On the bus ride home, I began counting down the hours until I'd be near him again and wondered if he and his companion would be gallant enough to come help us move our new stove and refrigerator on their preparation day.

With the back-and-forth to finalize a lease and arrange the move details, we saw each other every day for a week. The first couple days working together were thrilling; but the gnawing thought that my love life was supposed to be on hold dampened my excitement. I fasted to have platonic, missionary feelings for him. But the more I saw him in action and the more he helped me, the more I recognized qualities I wanted in my future husband—and my feelings for him swelled. It was probably just in my mind, but it seemed his grip grew stronger and somehow more heartfelt, shaking hands each day before my companion and I left the office. Now was not the time for this. By the end of the week, I had a nonstop queasy stomach, a pounding headache, and uncontrollably twitching eyelids and fingers. *At least after this week, I never have to go back to the office. Choir is over, and I'll just get back to my nice little missionary life and forget about him.*

When I met my new companion, Sister Peterson, she was filled with the Holy Ghost, almost aglow. She reminded me of myself leaving the MTC, but better. She was going to be a powerful missionary. As Elder Thompson and his companion drove us and her luggage to our new place, Elder Thompson mentioned that this was his last time helping out with a transfer, because he'd be leaving the office in a week.

"Oh yeah, where are you being transferred to?" I asked, looking at him in the rear-view mirror, sure he'd be sent to the struggling zone eight hours south. Sister Peterson's disappointment that we were speaking in English was palpable.

"Pres. decided to send me to this zone—I'll be in the area right next to you guys."

My heart flip-flopped: was this the best thing that could happen, or the absolute worst?

That evening Sister Peterson quickly fell asleep after we

prayed together, but my mind was racing as I tossed and turned. *How can I possibly train her?* "*See that ye serve him with all your heart, might, mind and strength, that ye may stand blameless before God at the last day.*" *I need to serve God with ALL my heart, not have some of it pining after an elder.* I couldn't fathom how I'd survive the twitterpation and my accompanying mental anguish at zone meeting on Tuesday, district meeting on Saturday, and at church on Sunday. *I'm here to do the Lord's work. Squelch these feelings for him!* I shuddered—*What if he'd been hoping to be transferred to my zone? I'd be unimpressed. Angry. That'd be a decisive step off the Super Missionary Pedestal I've put him on and into the mire.* And that's how I felt about myself—devoid of self-mastery and self-respect, flailing in the quicksand of infatuation.

I tried to pray mightily like Enos, pleading for forgiveness and help to regain focus on the Lord's work, until restless sleep finally overcame me.

The next morning, while my companion attended the orientation for new missionaries, I stared numbly at a picture of Christ in the mission office until I figured out what I could do for the next couple of hours—*study the scriptures, of course.* I searched for scriptures in English and finally spied black leather ones on a bookshelf, with a name engraved in gold in the bottom right-hand corner: Elder Michael Thompson. *Ironic. I'm seeking peace from my infatuation with him by borrowing his scriptures. Oh well.* He was explaining mission policies and didn't notice me heading for the supply closet to be alone. I flipped randomly, looking for anything to help my head stop spinning and quell the sick-to-my-stomach feeling. He'd marked his scriptures well and written so many personal notes in the margins that it was almost too intimate. I felt like I was looking into his honorable soul—and my guilt surged. I decided to read my favorite verses from 2 Nephi 4. The words that I'd loved for years seemed alarmingly relevant: "Why should my heart weep and my soul linger in the valley of sorrow. . . . And why should I yield to sin, because of my flesh? Yea, why should I give way to temptations, that the evil one have place in my heart to destroy my peace and afflict my soul?"

Nephi must have written this just for me—I think I understand his despondence at lingering in the valley of sorrow. What was my sin? Looking? Realizing we'd be perfect together? Being too cheerful around him? These all point to the same thing: unlocking my heart. There's no one moment that I did anything really sinful—but the sum of all the little things has destroyed my peace and afflicted my soul. I need help, Heavenly Father.

"O Lord, wilt thou redeem my soul? Wilt thou deliver me out of the hands of mine enemies? Wilt thou make me that I may shake at the appearance of sin? . . . O Lord, wilt thou encircle me around in the robe of thy righteousness! O Lord, wilt thou make a way for my escape before mine enemies!"

I need to escape. O Lord, wilt thou redeem my soul?

★ ★ ★ ★ ★

That night, I fasted for courage and strength. After playing the postlude at the mission conference the next day, I pulled President aside in the atrium.

"Could I talk with you for a minute, President?" My voice came out a little trembly.

"Of course, Sister Gates. How can I help you? Is everything going well training your new missionary?"

"Yes, she's wonderful . . . it's something else. I'm not quite sure how to say this, but . . ." I took a deep breath and tried to make eye contact, and then the words just tumbled out. "I'm really struggling to focus—I have a huge crush on Elder Thompson. I heard that he's coming to be my zone leader next week, but I was wondering if you could instead keep us in separate zones for the last few months of his mission."

President snapped to attention and rose to his full height. His bushy eyebrows shot up and his eyes opened almost as wide as his glasses. I succumbed to a sudden urge to examine my shoes. I felt his gaze, so I looked up with tears in my eyes. In a low voice he prodded, "Is there anything else you need to tell me?"

"Nope, that's it." I laughed, relieved, and a little bemused that he worried that something had actually happened. "I'm really sorry."

He relaxed a little, but not enough to smile. "These things happen, Sister Gates. Thanks for confiding in me. I'll think about the situation and decide what to do." He strode away purposefully toward the line of missionaries waiting by the CES office for interviews.

My heart felt light and clean. I practically skipped off to find my companion and get back to work establishing Zion.

★ ★ ★ ★ ★

The new zone leader the next week was Elder Santos. Everyone else was shocked it wasn't Elder Thompson. My best poker face hid my elation, but I had to dash to the restroom when tears of joy and relief snuck out. I heard he was shipped to a city four hours away.

I got a note from President a week later. He thanked me for my efforts to focus on my mission and said that my determination to be righteous would serve me well in this life and the next. *A clean slate feels so good.*

Sister Peterson and I spent only six weeks together, but it was a blissful and fruitful companionship. We witnessed several miracles together, and as I strove to give the work, the people, and the Lord all my heart, might, mind, and strength, I caught a glimpse of the joy of living a life consecrated to God and building His kingdom.

★ ★ ★ ★ ★

A year after I asked for President's help, I saw Mike Thompson again. I was in Salt Lake for a reunion and I'd asked him if we could go to dinner together. I needed closure. Small talk occupied the ride to the restaurant; then as we sat across the table from each other, I started to check for all those qualities I'd found so irresistible: good looks, intelligence, hard worker, spiritually alive, fun to talk with—yes, check, check, check. But . . . he wasn't quite my type—that was clear now. *Why the change?* Perhaps back on the mission I had succumbed to righteous-man-in-uniform syndrome. After all, now that Elder Thompson was wearing jeans and brown flip-flops but no name tag, the mantle of authority was gone. Maybe without missionary work as the shared focus of our lives, we had less in common. At any rate, I was extremely grateful that I hadn't wasted any more of the Lord's time, after Nephi's psalm had inspired and empowered me to seek help from my mission president and relock my heart.

When he finally dropped me off at my car and moved to hug me at the end of the evening, I stuck out my hand instead.

"Great to see you again, Thompson," I said, shaking his hand.

"Yup," he responded, without winking.

"Have a nice life." I grinned, relieved that it was really, finally over.

"You too, Gates." He gave me a fist bump.

And then I drove away from the man who had once been my own personal stumbling block. The one with the Harrison Ford smile.

Cloudy Days in Tacoma
Andrea Stradling Norton

ow-looming clouds covered the Washington sky all winter, and the specks of rain sometimes turned into thin mist. The spring was coming so the rain wasn't cold, but we were always wet. We had been trying to keep the missionary work alive, but it was hard not to let the constant drizzle outside reflect on our efforts.

I had been in the state of Washington for six months when I arrived in Tacoma for my first winter as a missionary. Here, I was partnered with two good-hearted sisters who respected me even though they had a lot more experience than I did. They knew me by reputation. When I had first come to the Evergreen State, I was full of fire, happy to work at a fast-paced beat in the Lord's vineyard to meet high expectations.

By the time I was serving in Tacoma, though, I wasn't sure I could sustain the energy and rate at which I was working. I had arrived in the heart of the mission, and we were supposed to be the example to everyone else. When Tacoma missionaries baptized, so did others in areas throughout the state. For whatever reason, others seemed to be dependent on the faith of the Tacoma missionaries. They were supposed to be a light to all the others, the most devoted to missionary work, and now I was one of them. We set a goal in our zone to work diligently and baptize a record-breaking number for the area, and even though everyone else seemed enthusiastic about it, I felt disconnected.

In addition to this load of expectation, the other sisters and I felt an extra weight on our shoulders from the ward leaders who needed us to help recently baptized members. I quickly learned that our ward, unlike some of the others in the area, was struggling in member activity and retention, especially among recent converts. We met on a weekly basis with our ward mission leader, who was supposed to be our advocate. I sensed his doubt in our motives. He had been exposed to missionaries who were there with the sole purpose of never letting the font go dry. Although baptism is a central focus of missionary work, this ward mission leader had lost trust in the quality of conversions that came from past missionaries. The missionaries' urgency and drive scared ward members and created a wall between their collaborative efforts. Our ward mission leader looked at me the same way he looked at the ones before me—a missionary who was only there to find, teach, baptize, and move on to the next contestant, never to look back again. Was that who I was? Did I have room in my heart to love these people and serve them as Christ would?

Outside pressures aside, I still wasn't feeling great. The constant dismal clouds represented missionary work to me: never-ending. Study, work, sleep, repeat. I began to slip in my energy as a missionary, and I found myself going through the motions without feeling the importance of my actions. The appeal of sleep seemed more rewarding than anything else at 6:30 in the morning, and my eyelids weighed heavily as I faced the daily chore of studying the scriptures. I tried to fight the drowsiness, but the disconnected verses provided only small traces of spiritual power and strength throughout the day. I wrestled for words as we taught lessons. My mouth would open, but the words would choke in my throat as I spoke them, as if I were suffocating, struggling for air to breathe. One rule for all the missionaries was to tract every night from five to seven, and two hours each night of knocking on door after door became a burden. With the way I was feeling, what was I supposed to say? "Hello, my name is Sister Stradling, the scripted missionary robot, would you like to learn about our church?" I didn't want to be on autoplay; I wanted to care for these people, I wanted to be sincere. But I just couldn't feel much of anything: no love, no joy, no hope. How long could I go on like this? The pressure from others' expectations began to haunt me, and I wondered if I was really as uncaring as the ward mission leader perceived me to be.

My fire of enthusiasm had dwindled to a mere pile of smoldering ashes, which I barely kept burning. Even my family perceived that I was not the same. "Are you okay?" my mother asked in response to my email home. She knew that something was wrong and that I wasn't happy. The truth was that I felt like a failure. I couldn't wake up in the morning, read the scriptures, or arrive at appointments on time. I couldn't recognize the Spirit or feel my Savior's love. How was I supposed to help someone else when I couldn't even help myself?

On Tuesday morning, we went to our weekly missionary meeting at the church. As we pulled up to the chapel, anxiety stirred inside of me. I put on a smile as we entered the building, trying to hide the burden I carried. We exchanged pleasantries with other missionaries, and I headed straight for my seat, avoiding unnecessary conversations, and putting on my all-business face. I stared at the chalkboard, which was covered with the large missionary reporting chart. Missionary companionships were listed down the chart with "Sisters" about half way down the list. I scrambled to grab my planner and look at the numbers again, even though I knew what they were.

As the meeting started, missionaries took their turns reporting the progress from the past week, and there seemed to be a celebration for the accomplishments of all of them. Our turn was next. "Sisters?" There was a pause. I dreaded what was to come next: "Zero baptisms, zero at church . . ." As I continued to report our numbers, I wondered what they were thinking. "What are those sisters doing? Have they been working at all?" The thick silence was broken by words of encouragement from the other missionaries, which helped me to keep my composure. But I began to wonder, did I have enough faith in the Lord and confidence in myself to be an instrument in facilitating miracles? I stared at the ground and avoided all eye contact throughout the rest of the meeting.

I suspected that my leaders knew I was struggling, but what could they do? They had their work to do, and I had mine. I needed help, but who could help me? One day, while waiting for interviews with our mission president at the church building, another missionary asked me if I would play some interlude music. The hymn book fell open to "Abide with Me" as I headed toward the piano. While my fingers touched the keys, playing the familiar notes, my eyes wandered to the lyrics. "The darkness deepens. Lord, with me abide!" Where was the Lord during my hours of darkness? "I need thy presence every passing hour. . . . Thru cloud and sunshine, Lord, abide with me!" The words became blurry. Where was the light and hope that came from my Savior?

Before I knew it, my turn to speak with the mission president was next. I tried to clear my face and act as if everything was normal. I knew he was a representative of God, full of love, but in that moment, I did not wax confident in his sight. He called my name, and I entered the room, sitting across the table from him.

"How are you doing, Sister Stradling?"

"I'm doing okay." He could discern something was wrong.

"How are things with your companions?"

"They are good." He knew this was something deeper than a companionship disagreement.

"What can I do to help you?"

With a trembling voice and tear-filled eyes, I extended my hand through thin air, hoping to find something physical to touch. "I know my Savior is there, I just can't feel Him."

He looked at me patiently and with reassurance, as if wanting to take away my pain.

"Know that God loves you," he said confidently. "Overcome second thoughts and feelings of doubt with feelings of the Spirit."

He tried to reassure me as he told me that the Savior was there, but he knew that as my mission president he couldn't overcome these trials of discouragement and depression for me. I had been blessed with the Spirit in so many moments throughout my life, but why couldn't I recognize the promptings now?

I went back to work, hoping that my mission president was right. My life as a missionary still seemed monotonous, laborious, and ineffective: study, doors, rain, and rejection, day after day. But in striving to follow the mission president's counsel, we worked to build unity with the members through the "One Church" initiative by "ward listing." One night during our planning session, we stared at the ward list. *Who should we go see?* I wondered as we turned page after page. Out of about 350 families on the list, an average of 60 people had been attending our Sunday meetings. There were so many names we didn't recognize, and so many people we had never met. The name *Eric Lake* stood out to us, a young man, who was the only one listed in his family.

After knocking on doors until dusk the next day, we set out to find Eric Lake. We followed the map and turned onto Gunnison

Street, slowing the car to a crawl until we found the right house number. We parked in front of a small, bluish-gray structure that blended in with the gloomy Washington sky. It was a modest home covered in wooden slats, and on the small porch sat one single white plastic chair, matching the white trim of the house. Our shoes clacked on the cement path that cut the unkempt yard in half. I began to have an uneasy feeling. We stepped up the three damp stairs that led to the door and saw the pile of cigarette butts in the corner of the porch. Either Eric needed the Lord's help in his life, or he wasn't prepared to return to His fold, and we were about to find out. The screen door squeaked as I opened it slowly. We gave our cheerful-rhythmic knock, hoping to lighten any opposition we might face. A middle-aged, average-height woman opened the door, letting the dim light of her house escape. It smelled of rose petals, soft and easy, mixed with a strong scent of coffee. Her bushy, brown hair came past her shoulders and rested on her dress suit, which looked as tired as her worn face. I wondered if she, too, carried a burden.

"Is Eric here?" we asked.

"No, he's not," she replied with ease and curiosity.

"Well, we're just here from The Church of Jesus Christ of Latter-day Saints, and we came to visit him. Eric was on our roll, and we were wondering how he's doing."

The lady seemed confused. "Eric is my son. I didn't know he was a member of your church." She informed us that her older son, Eric, had moved out a while ago. "What church did you say you were from?"

"The Church of Jesus Christ of Latter-day Saints." We seized the opportunity for an invitation, "We're doing tours of our church building tomorrow night or Monday night. Would you like to come down and check it out at 7:00?" She hesitated, and then a scruffy voice bellowed above the background noise of the TV, "Tell them I'm sick." She explained that her husband had an illness that prevented him from going out often, but she agreed to bring her younger son, Donny, to tour the church on Monday night.

"Okay! What's your name?" we asked as I held my breath with excitement, hoping that we found a new investigator.

"Mara," she gently replied. We promptly wrote her name down in our planner for Monday at 7:00. We promised her that she would find what she was looking for and left her our card with an appointment reminder, feeling that we had accomplished what we were sent there to do.

As Monday rolled around, we went about business as usual. We had invited a couple from the congregation, the Stringhams, to join us for the appointment with Mara and Donny. This was mostly wishful thinking because in the past, investigators had almost never shown up for appointments to see the church. Before the scheduled tour, we spent our time knocking on doors.

Right as we finished our last door at 7:00, our phone rang. It was Sister Stringham, wondering where on earth we were. She informed us that she and her husband were at the church with Mara Lake and her son Donny, waiting for us to get there. We felt a zing of excitement as we reassured her that we were on our way, and we jumped in our car to speed off to the church house.

Upon arrival, we exchanged pleasantries, apologized for being late, and headed to unlock the door of the church. As Mara and the rest followed us down the hallway of the church, we asked her why she had come on the tour, hoping to discover what had motivated her to learn about our church.

"I've been feeling a void in my life," she replied slowly, "and was hoping that this might fill it somehow." I realized that she was genuinely seeking hope and truth, someone in need of the Lord's help. I couldn't be on autopilot this time. I needed to teach with the Spirit and with love.

We walked around the different parts of our church, identifying the pictures of Christ, the chapel, and the baptism font. The Stringhams shared powerful testimonies and invited Mara and Donny to join them for sacrament meeting. As we concluded the tour, we all sat down for a lesson, and the time came for me to share my part. If there was any spiritual strength left in me, this was the time to use it.

"Mara, there was once a young boy who had a void, like you. And, like you, he was searching for the true church." I proceeded to tell her the story of Joseph's study, his prayer, and vision: "I saw a pillar of light, exactly over my head, above the brightness of the sun, which descended gradually until it fell upon me . . ." The Spirit was tangible, but could I feel it? I wanted Mara to feel it, but I also wanted to experience the hope and peace. I had recounted this vision so many times, and I didn't want to feel numb to the power of its truthfulness. Despite my internal conflict, when Mara learned how God answered Joseph's prayer, appearing to him and calling him by name, she found the answer to her own prayer. Like a child whose parents call after her to come home, she was starting to recognize the beckoning of her Heavenly Father. The Spirit was so thick and influential that even though I could not recognize it in the moment, Mara Lake felt something, and she knew she did. The Stringhams felt it too. After listening to the story, Mara told us of her feelings of relief. She was working late hours because she was the sole provider for her family, caring for her ill husband, dealing with children making poor choices, and searching for her own truth and light. But Mara felt the hope that comes from the Savior and the strength to continue through her trials. I extended the invitation of baptism, but it felt surreal, as if I were looking down on the situation and not fully understanding the impact of that kind of commitment.

I was drained by the time we finished our tour and lesson, exhausted from focusing my spiritual and emotional energy. Even so, I found myself thinking about Mara, wondering whether she would push through obstacles in her path and receive the fulness of the gospel.

She came to church the following Sunday and sat by the Stringhams. This began her journey of faith, which included scripture study, prayer, application of the gospel principles, and quitting coffee. A couple of weeks after her first lesson, Mara was ready and committed to being baptized. One Sunday night, we entered the Relief Society room where the baptism was to be held, and I could hear the rush of pounding water filling up the font behind the curtains.

Mara showed up with her son Donny, who was also going to be baptized. She was wearing her typical dress pants and suit coat, her outfit for special occasions. We guided Mara to the clothing closet to pick out her white baptism dress, held up a few options, and found one that fit her just right. Dressed in white, she was ready to go down into the waters of baptism. After she came up out of the water, not only did Mara feel relieved, but I did too.

Our mission motto included the phrase "Joy is the Reward," but at the time of Mara's baptism, I felt only a teaspoonful of joy in my heart. This was all that I needed in the moment to sustain me through my trials of discouragement. Even though I still struggled to overcome my feelings of duty-driven missionary work and depression, I saw Mara as a source of hope. Hope for me. If she was stalwart in her trials and willing to make changes, I knew that through the Atonement of Jesus Christ, I would be able to make it through my difficulties. She was an example to me of how rain didn't have to rust away at my soul; it could actually cleanse and renew my outlook on life. For me, this came as I was able to work through my struggles and complete an honorable mission about a year later.

I did not feel the full joy that came from serving in Tacoma until I had already finished my missionary service. One warm, summer evening, Mara called me up, reporting that a couple of weeks later she would be going to the temple. I just about dropped the phone. She, a product of the most difficult period of my mission and a member of the lowest-retaining ward, would be my first convert to go through the temple! I jumped at the opportunity to take a road trip to Washington so I could be with her while she made more important covenants with Heavenly Father. When that Saturday morning came, we arrived at the temple, and once again, Mara changed into a white dress. A feeling of gratitude and love overcame me.

At the end of our temple experience, Mara introduced me to the others who had come. "This is the sister missionary who came and knocked on my door—thanks so much for coming!" I burst into tears at these words, and we embraced, holding each other for a few moments that felt like eternity. She couldn't have looked more perfect, and the happiness and love that radiated from her poured into my heart and throughout my entire body. In that minute, everything was worth it—all the rain, the freezing cold fingers knocking on doors, the feelings of doubt and inadequacy—all of it was worth it for that moment.

Even though I never actually met Eric Lake, I knew that we had been guided by the Spirit to find Mara. I realize now that despite my weaknesses, by relying on my Savior Jesus Christ and being obedient, the Lord will always shower us with miracles. He is the way to find hope and renewal, not only for the investigators, but also for me.

ANDREA STRADLING NORTON, daughter of Keith and Dianna Stradling, grew up in Mesa, Arizona. After completing her degree in elementary education at Northern Arizona University, she served a mission under President Kent Bowen. Andrea taught school in Utah where she met her husband. Layne and Andrea Norton reside in Lubbock, Texas, where Andrea is completing a master's degree in educational leadership at Lubbock Christian University.

Using Optimism as a Shield
Sarah Tanner Briggs

Before I even arrived in Korea, I met my mission president in the MTC. He had come for the orientation for new mission presidents, an event which filled the hallways of the MTC with anticipation and excitement. As missionaries, meeting our new mission presidents was better than meeting any celebrity. I automatically assumed that President Cho and I were going to be the best of friends. Why would it be any other way?

I was walking to lunch with my district when I spotted him—a small Asian man standing in the hallway with his wife. Without waiting for logic to catch up with my excitement, I dropped my ten-pound stack of scriptures and flashcards and broke into a full-on sprint in his direction. What was that look on his face as I approached? Bewilderment? Unfazed, I threw my arms around this man and hugged him with all my might. Thank heavens I did not knock him to the ground. His body and his arms stayed glued to his side, hard as stone, and they never softened. His sweet wife eventually touched my side and directed my energy into her embrace, relieving her husband of this stunning first encounter. I learned later that in Korea, President Cho's native country, even looking a stranger in the eye could be seen as an invasion of privacy. Husband and wife rarely hug in public, and there I was, a twenty-one-year-old girl, trying to hug a strange man. However disrespectful of authority my actions were in their culture, my optimism about serving the Lord in Korea shone through. It created a bond between us that stuck throughout the mission and he referred to me as his 장녀 (first born daughter) because of the incident.

My mission president and I struggled to speak to each other my entire mission. He began our very first interview together by reeling off a few sentences in Korean. I smiled but didn't respond. He then nodded, as if to say, "Oh, I see you do not understand," and spoke the same sentences more slowly, only to receive my same smile with a little shoulder shrug. He simplified and slowed down his speech several times before we both finally realized that despite my efforts to learn Korean in the MTC, I could not understand a single word. So he finally used the few English words he knew. "Happy?"

I responded, "Yes."

"Good," he said, with a thumbs up. Then he said, "Go," and I turned around and left.

I could have felt discouraged, which would have slowed my momentum going into the mission field. Instead I decided to feel inspired, for the same reason sleeping on the floor and eating kimchi at every meal was inspiring. I was going to do something really hard and love it. My dad used to walk into a room of grumpy kids, clap his hands and say, "Let's do it!" He had a way of energizing any crowd (while embarrassing his kids) and turning a challenge into an adventure. He used to write notes of encouragement and stick them on the bathroom mirror. Thirteen years after his death, the one that remains reads: "Do it, and then some!" On my mission, this saying reminded me that there was so much good to be done. I needed to "do it" instead of fretting about the things that made me uncomfortable. I think of my father's mother who put on a happy face and said, "Hello, Hello, Hello. What a marvelous day! I am what

I am, what a great thing to be, if I say so myself, happy everyday to me." Raising fourteen kids on a meager income with an abusive husband brought disappointment and hurt, but my grandmother's fierce positive attitude allowed her to progress. The optimism that she and my father embraced came from the Atonement. I knew from their examples that even in the middle of a challenge, like a language barrier that made it hard for my mission president to understand or communicate with me, I had reason to hope.

The power of optimism helped me during one of the darkest moments on my mission. My companion was struggling with an eating disorder and became severely depressed. We were united in our testimony of the gospel, but somehow we didn't know how to pull ourselves out of this dark hole. We needed momentum to latch on to the rope that would pull us out. We would continually study together and pray together, but the cracks of sunlight came only when she would tap dance in the elevator or I would click my heels before we knocked on another door. These were simple signs of saying, "Good is going to come." And it did. I could almost see the dark fog clear when she would perform "The Sun Will Come Out Tomorrow" from *Annie* in the kitchen of our apartment. It was as if our actions were sending a message to the other side: we will see the good in the world and will not be overcome. In retrospect, I recognize tapping your heels won't solve depression, but I did feel power in our positive actions. They enabled us to grab on to a lifeline of healing and hope.

President Gordon B. Hinckley said, "We have every reason to be optimistic in this world. . . . Tragedy is around, yes. Problems everywhere, yes. . . . You can't, you don't, build out of pessimism or cynicism. You look with optimism, work with faith, and things happen."[12]

---

12 Jeffrey R. Holland, "President Gordon B. Hinckley, Stalwart and Brave He Stands," *Ensign*, June 1995, 4.

I used the shield of optimism to protect against the rejection, exhaustion, and depression that can accompany missionary work. Optimism can protect you from darkness. It can pull you to the sunlight where things grow.

SARAH TANNER BRIGGS gradu-  ated from BYU in recreational therapy. Shortly after, she married her childhood sweetheart and moved to Boston. She now has two children and blogs at PlayWithYourFamily .com, a website that encourages families to strengthen their relationships through play. She believes almost all the good in life is learned through play, and she dreams of one day opening her own family therapy practice in her backyard.

Building Zion One
Brick at a Time

Deborah Petersen Nash

When my mission president told me that I would be transferred, I was incredulous. It was happening once again to me, the official sister-nomad of the Switzerland Zürich Mission. There were always good reasons for the transfers, of course. In one area, my companion and I found a previous investigator who confused the feeling of the Holy Spirit with a feeling of infatuation with me. He started to stalk us, and I was transferred out of the area in a hurry. Another time, President assigned me to replace a senior couple that suddenly needed to go home. Most sisters in my mission served in only two or three areas during their eighteen months. With this last transfer, I was up to six. Besides, I was sad to leave area five, which had been bursting with investigators. We had built up the largest teaching pool in the mission, and I didn't think I would ever again find so many listeners.

If I could have, I would have stayed put a little longer, building that one corner of Zion with a craftsman's precision until the job was done, but my mission required me to learn how to build Zion one brick here, another brick there, piecing the city of God together in different ways and different places. I had to find peace with that. And it became clear to me that my contribution in my next area would be very different from what I had given before.

"... They Were of One Heart and One Mind ..."

My new companion and I had met previously, but we hadn't worked much together during our missions. She was friendly and adorable—that much I knew before we met—and she possessed strong faith in miracles. I quickly discovered that she also worried too much and had a hard time slowing down. She felt compelled to work hard, often at the expense of herself and those around her, and it was wearing her thin. She needed to slow down and move at a more sustainable pace.

My companion worked hard and contacted people constantly. One morning as we were knocking doors, I looked at my watch and told her we needed to head to the bus stop. "Just a couple more. You never know who we might find," she said. Nobody answered that door or the next. We watched the bus pass by the stop.

"So we missed our bus," I said. "We should leave now to catch the next one. If we miss that one, we'll have to walk to get to our next appointment, and we'll be late." She insisted on knocking even more doors while we waited for the next bus to arrive. I urged her to "see that all these things are done in wisdom and order; for it is not requisite that a man should run faster than he has strength" (Mosiah 4:27). It was an argument that I had been using more and more with her lately.

She responded, "I am going to knock on another door. I will not wait at a bus stop." Of course, we missed the next bus. But when we started walking the long distance to our next appointment, Sister Meyer, a member of our ward, drove around the corner and waved to us, allowed us to flag her down, and then cheerfully allowed us to ride in her car to our appointment.

I'll admit, I felt slightly annoyed. Sister Meyer had just rescued us from being late and walking a long way, which meant my companion wouldn't learn her lesson about pushing too hard. But then I began to think about it a little more. Was it better to set unrealistic goals that required a miracle of the Lord to attain, or to act with reason and not require a miracle in the first place? I concluded that both approaches were necessary. In my mission journal, I wrote, "We are not perfect people. We all have different needs. We have to work together! . . . When we fall, others learn to lift, and when they fall, we learn to lift them. The best thing about working together is that you have to learn how to work together."

My companion lifted me with her faith, and I learned that I could lift her by helping her to be reasonable with her limitations. It was one of the purposes of our companionship, I realized. She needed me to help her stop spreading herself thin. In order to ease the tension and to unify us, I suggested that we set a superordinate goal. It needed to be an attainable one—a goal that would help her to focus without wearing herself down, and a goal that wouldn't take any extra time. Our mission had a rule that we should always speak in German when we were outside our apartments. Although both my companion and I sincerely wanted to improve our ability to speak German, neither of us followed this rule very closely. We gave it prayerful consideration and set a goal to speak only German both inside and outside the apartment.

The goal wasn't as easy as it might seem. All missionaries called to the Zürich mission were called to speak German; however, the Swiss people do not speak traditional high German as their native language. On a typical day of street contacting, I could come prepared with a Book of Mormon in German and pamphlets in English, Albanian, and Croatian, and end up making contacts with people from Iraq, Africa, and Russia. As missionaries, we routinely promised to search out materials in different languages for interested investigators.

Fortunately, both my companion and I were both experienced missionaries with a solid grasp on the language, so the goal wasn't too far of a stretch. By the afternoon of the first day, we were already cracking jokes in German. Nobody else thought our jokes were funny, but we laughed so hard we cried. The goal unified us and helped us become of one heart and one mind. I wanted to be obedient. I wanted to nurture my companion's drive and determination, but I also wanted to respect her physical limitations. I felt that this combination of striving for unification and loving each other, despite our weaknesses, brought the Spirit into our companionship, allowing us to feel a piece of Zion in our hearts.

". . . And Dwelt in Righteousness . . ."

With this particular companion, our efforts led to obvious results that I could experience immediately—more unity, more joy. In other cases, my righteous efforts to build the kingdom of God didn't seem to go anywhere.

Just prior to my arrival in a new city, Sister Maughan had knocked on the door of Ms. Thoma. Ms. Thoma answered that door and said "I've been waiting for you!" Confused, the sisters asked her if she knew who they were. Ms. Thoma explained that she was familiar with the Church and had been waiting for missionaries to find her.

After a conversation on the doorstep, Sister Maughan set up an appointment for a formal discussion. When she and her companion returned to teach the lesson, Ms. Thoma was not there. Later when I started working in the area, each time we returned, no one answered the door. We left notes and brochures anyway. Normally we would have stopped knocking on her door, but we felt a spiritual push to keep returning. Sister Maughan felt strongly about Ms. Thoma's potential.

Sister Maughan and I continued to drop by on Ms. Thoma, hoping that we could reconnect with her. One time, she was actually there. As soon as I met her, I understood why Sister Maughan hadn't given up on her. She physically looked like a golden contact with her blonde hair swooped above her shoulders and her countenance radiating light. She seemed familiar to me because she reminded me of another member of our ward. I learned that even though she was born in Switzerland, Ms. Thoma spoke articulate English after spending several years in Canada earning a theology degree.

We walked into her quaint townhouse, which felt homey and surprisingly spacious. Sister Maughan and I taught her about the First Vision. She loved it. We all felt the Spirit. Ms. Thoma agreed to a second appointment without hesitation, and we couldn't wait to teach the next discussion. Our persistence in contacting her over the weeks seemed to be paying off.

Sister Nisson, fresh from another area, accompanied me for the much-anticipated discussion. We taught about repentance and baptism, and Ms. Thoma seriously considered the message. She brought up all sorts of questions from her study of the Book of Mormon. As the discussion progressed, she sensed where this was leading: a baptismal invitation. I could tell that she knew the power of the commitment, but she just wasn't ready to answer the question. Still, we left with light hearts and a third appointment scheduled.

When we arrived at her apartment for that third appointment, the door didn't open. Ms. Thoma returned to the pattern of avoiding us. She was never home, she never responded, and I never got to teach her again. In all, I spent five months leaving notes on her door. Under typical circumstances, it wouldn't have made sense to go back more than two or three times. Yet we knew that she was different.

My time on the mission ran out before I was able to see her again. Sister Nisson was assigned to take over the area. Even after arriving home, I prayed for Ms. Thoma regularly and never stopped trying to make contact with her. I was amazed, a couple months later, when Sister Nisson wrote to tell me that Ms. Thoma had contacted the missionaries to say that she finally felt ready to be baptized. She had just needed time to prepare herself for this life change. Even before her baptism, she started holding family home evenings with her two teenage daughters.

I wrote Ms. Thoma to congratulate her. She told me that if it hadn't been for all those reminders, she would have allowed herself to forget what she knew. Many missionaries' habits of righteousness—persistence, prayer, and unity—kept Sister Thoma on the path of change and conversion. The Architect of Zion had been carefully directing our efforts the entire time. Though our efforts might have looked disjointed and unpromising, they led Sister Thoma back to the fold so that she could "dwell in righteousness" once again with the Lord.

I knew that the Swiss Saints would take good care of Sister Thoma because they had taken good care of so many others, even members who came from different circumstances.

". . . And There Was No Poor among Them . . ."

Switzerland attracts people from all over the world because of its wealth. The Swiss people use their abundance for good by establishing refugee asylums throughout the country, where people from troubled nations can find their footing. The asylums are permanent structures, like dormitories, where a guard stands watch at the door. Each asylum has a community kitchen, bathrooms, and common spaces. Refugees are given a small allowance for food, clothing, or other needs. The situation makes for fairly comfortable living, but nothing desirable in the long term. Most refugees are African males, some who survived terrible wars, and others who are simply hoping to improve their lives in a more established country.

Between our walk from the apartment to the church in one of my areas sat one of these refugee asylums. Two of our branch members lived there, so we were able to get to know other residents. Within a few weeks, we had about fifteen men regularly attending church and we were teaching our own Sunday School class in English. The refugees were humble because of their situation. Their lives were difficult, but they seemed to maintain a sense of their intrinsic worth and a strong faith in God. They had very little to offer, and yet what they had, they offered freely.

While checking up on an investigator in one of our city's three refugee asylums, a man named Peter Ngugu approached us. "I'm very religious," he said, "and I want to talk to you!" We didn't know what to say. It was hard to know if he was sincere. "I'm looking for a congregation," he went on. "Not a baptism, just a congregation."

He started to listen as I explained how he could learn even more about Jesus Christ by studying what other prophets have written about Him. I explained the Book of Mormon. When I said that Christ had appeared in America after His death, Peter looked as though he'd seen an angel.

"Can I read this book myself?"

Smiling, I gave him a copy of the book and answered, "Of course."

Several times over the next few weeks, we tried to teach Peter about the First Vision, but we never met as scheduled. We were only able to have little conversations whenever we happened to bump into him. When I left the area, I continued to pray for him as he studied and learned the truths of the Book of Mormon.

Several months later, I came back to that area to sing and play the piano for a baptism. I was amazed to see Peter there—strong in faith! He stood at the pulpit and bore testimony that this Church is true, and that he was grateful for his "favorite missionary" who was able to get him to listen. I was so touched that he remembered me and had built his testimony upon what I had taught him.

Teaching Peter and other refugees reminded me of something the Savior said in the New Testament: "Blessed are the poor in spirit: for theirs is the kingdom of heaven" (Matthew 5:3). I felt the truth of these words. These refugees were poor, yes. They were poor in spirit. But as they sought the Lord whose name I bore on my name tag, I felt the richness of the Spirit overflowing within me. The kingdom of heaven felt closer and I felt the external lines of financial disparity blur and disappear as we taught of Christ. "There were not rich and poor . . . but they were all . . . partakers of the heavenly gift" (4 Nephi 1:3).

★ ★ ★ ★ ★

I had to learn how to build the Lord's kingdom a little here, a little there. Notes, pamphlets, lessons, prayers, friendship—I placed all these bricks in scattered corners of the kingdom of God during my mission in Switzerland, and I couldn't see much of a pattern. When I look back now, though, I can see a shining "City of Holiness, even Zion" (Moses 7:19) that's stronger and fuller than before.

These memories are dedicated to Sister Whitni Nisson Reese, 1981–2011. Great shall be your joy.

DEBORAH PETERSEN NASH was raised in Salt Lake City, Utah. She earned a bachelor's in art history at The College of William and Mary in Williamsburg, Virginia. She worked for the city of Annapolis, Maryland, and then she earned a master's degree in business administration from the University of Utah. Deborah now works for Ancestry.com, travels abroad, and is happily married.

My Mission Heart Transplant

Jeanne Ensign Larson

I t was past bedtime, and I desperately wanted to be sleeping. My mind and body were exhausted as I lay under my covers in the dark, but I kept hearing a low, muffled noise. As I sat up to listen more intently, I could tell that it was my companion. She was crying. It sounded like a normal cry at first, but it quickly grew louder and more pained. She was sobbing. And then she started to speak to me. "I can't do it anymore." She took a deep breath, "I have tried and tried, but I can't do everything the way you want me to."

I sat still, not knowing how to act. The anguish she felt was seeping out of her in a flow of tears and deafening sobs. I had never heard anyone sound more miserable.

And I was the cause.

We had met in the Missionary Training Center where we were assigned to be companions. We were both called to serve in the Missouri Independence Mission, and we shared a common departure date. Three weeks of learning flew by, and we had since served in different areas in the field for seven months. When transfer calls came, I was moved to Manhattan, Kansas, to be reunited with her. She had already been serving there for over a month, so she was familiar with the area. I was excited to serve with her again. When I received this new assignment, I had a peaceful sense that I would learn a lot from her.

I jumped into the work. I scoured the area book for effective leads, contacted members for splits, and set out to tract during any cancellations or gaps between our appointments. I sought to accomplish our mission goals each day and each week. On a daily basis, without exception, we were expected to tract for two hours and contact at least twenty new people. I believed in tracting. It hadn't always been easy for me, a people pleaser by nature, but tracting had allowed me to meet the Fillmores in my first area. They were noble souls, hungry for truth. Lynette was the first to decide that she wanted to enter the waters of baptism. I still remember the tears in her eyes when she told us that she had received an answer. A week later, her husband, Dennis, called to tell us that he had received his own answer. He was baptized the following weekend. Meeting them made me want to go door to door in the cold to find others that may be searching as they had been. In addition to tracting, we missionaries were expected to teach a minimum of twenty-five discussions and invite at least three less-active members to meet with the bishop. These mission goals were my goals. If we needed to work through lunch or dinner or both to accomplish these things, I wanted to do it.

My companion never wanted to miss lunch, and she refused to cut the hour short. She needed her mid-day nap. She enjoyed working with less-actives, and she loved dining with the active members of the church. She felt a deep kinship with them, and I could tell right away that many of the members of the local ward considered her to be their friend. She had a natural love for them, and they felt it. Still, it was difficult to peel her away from their homes as the appointed hour drew to a close each evening. She lingered and chatted and wanted to stay. She also preferred just about any kind of missionary work to tracting. When we had holes in our schedule, I would pull out a map of the area to pray about what street we should tract. She would figure out what part of the city we were already in and finger through the flash cards of less active and active members who lived nearby. We could not have approached the work more differently. I was determined to prove to her that if we worked extra hard and were strictly obedient to mission rules, the Lord would bless us.

Each night, we were supposed to call our district leader to report on our progress with the work. This nightly phone call was known as accountability. At the end of each week, the accountability phone call included all of our numbers from the past week so that the mission office could keep track of what was happening in all the different areas: discussions taught, days that we made at least twenty contacts, less-actives invited to meet with the bishop, baptismal sets (or dates set for baptisms), as well as several other mission goals.

When it was my day to make the call, and I could feel my palms getting sweaty. I worried that if we did not achieve every single mission goal, it reflected poorly on me as a missionary. Of course, deep down, I knew better, but saying my failures out loud seemed to reinforce the feeling that I did not measure up. In my mind, I had set the district leader up as my judge, waiting to condemn any departure from mission rules. I took a deep breath.

"Sisters, how was your day?"

"It was good, Elder Jackson, how was yours?"

"Fabulous! We had some great discussions, and the Ramos family came to church this week! How has your week been? Do you have anyone set for baptism?"

"Not at this point." I cringed. We had not reached our goal for baptismal sets.

"How many discussions did you teach this week?"

"We taught twenty-seven!" I beamed.

"Wow! That's great, sisters! How many of them had members present?"

"We had members present at four of them, and three of them were taught in a member's home."

"Glad to hear it," he replied. "How did everything else go?"

"We met with three less-active members and invited them to meet with the bishop. We tracted and spoke with at least twenty new people each day this week except for yesterday." I hated to report any holes in our progress.

"What happened yesterday?"

"We ended up teaching a lot of discussions, so we had no time to tract," I said sheepishly.

"Well, you can always grab the phone book and call twenty people while you are driving between appointments."

"Okay, Elder."

"Well, keep trying sisters. Maybe if you work a bit harder you will be able to reach all of your goals next week!"

"Okay, Elder." I felt my cheeks growing hot.

"Have a good night!"

"Good night." I was fighting the tears back. I hated that.

I hung up the phone angry and ashamed. I don't think he was purposely trying to make me feel bad, but I was not accustomed to falling short on anything. My perceived inadequacies stung. I wanted to succeed. I wanted him to know that I could do everything that was asked of me.

I poured over our blue planning schedules. What could we do better? Where could we work harder? Where could we work smarter? Next week we would reach all of our goals; I was resolute. We could do it. We could be above reproach. All I needed to do was get my companion on board.

Only now, I knew that I had broken her.

I don't know how either of us managed to get any sleep that night. All I remember is that stabbing feeling. I was responsible for her suffering. In my quest to change her, I had crushed her. I had taken any hope, love, and energy she had for the work, and I had squelched it. Never before had I been the instrument of so much pain. How had I caused so much distress when my desire was for us to be good, obedient, hard-working missionaries? Where had I gone wrong?

The next morning I felt awkward and self-conscious around my companion, but breakfast and our morning study time proceeded as usual. I opened my scriptures to study the War in Heaven. I read about Satan's plan. "Behold, here am I, send me, I will be thy son, and I will redeem all mankind, that one soul shall not be lost, and surely I will do it; wherefore give me thine honor" (Moses 4:1). I noted how many times Satan referred to himself. I could hear my own voice in those words, "Behold, here am I, send me, I will be thy servant, and I will baptize all of thy children . . . surely I will do it; wherefore give me thine honor." I read on about the Savior's willingness to follow His Father's plan, "Father, thy will be done, and the glory be thine forever" (Moses 4:2). Not a single mention of Himself. Then I read this: "Wherefore, because that Satan rebelled against me, and sought to destroy the agency of man, which I, the Lord God, had given him, and also, that I should give unto him mine own power . . . I caused that he should be cast down" (Moses 4:3). I felt a surge of insight into the nature of the evil one. He was fueled by three main objectives: first, to do his own will and rebel against the Father; second, to destroy the agency of others; and third, to gain power, glory, and honor.

I didn't feel any desire to rebel against my Heavenly Father, but I definitely did want to control the agency of my companion. I felt that her level of obedience and effort reflected negatively on me. I wanted to make her walk out the door at 9:30 in the morning and not a minute later. I wanted to drag her along tracting through lunch instead of allowing her to sleep. Why did I want that so desperately? What did I hope to gain?

Then I thought about nightly accountability. I knew that the purpose of the phone call was simply to check in with my district leader, so that he knew we were okay and to send along information, but I had started to make more of these simple conversations. When it was my turn to make the call, I would worry about it all day unless I felt that I had something impressive to share. Was I really that concerned about being judged by a fellow missionary? Was his praise and respect more important than the well being of my poor companion? When it came down to it, was I more concerned with what people heard about me than what my Savior thought of me? The Spirit pressed on my heart like an anvil.

Agency. I wanted to take hers away. Honor. I wanted it from everyone. The source of these two base desires was the adversary, not the Savior. The impression was soft, yet piercing: by attempting to control my companion for the sake of my own recognition and glory, I was acting more like Satan than like the Savior. The Spirit's message for me was clear and direct. I hit my knees. "Father, please help me. I am so sorry. I am hurting Thy daughter—my companion—and I don't want her to hurt anymore. Please help me change! I don't know how. I want to stop caring what anyone thinks of me. I want to feel Thy love for her. I want to have Thy help to do Thy work. I don't want to be driven by numbers and motivated by outside recognition. Please help me to have a new heart, a pure heart, a changed heart."

We continued to labor together, and weeks passed. As time went by, I started to get the impression that we should stop tracting in our current area, but I fought it. How would we find people to teach? How could we reach our goals and teach discussions if we did not tract? How would my district leader know that we were working hard if we did not do what was expected? Each time we would pick a street and start to knock on doors, I would feel uneasy, like a child who was doing something her parent had asked her not to. Yet I would persist, to my discomfort. I wanted to tract. We were supposed to tract!

I was determined to be obedient to our mission rules, so I ignored the feeling that directed us otherwise. My companion shared this same sense as well, but I assumed that she just didn't want to tract because I knew how much she disliked it. However, the feeling continued to bear down on us over time.

After several days of this, the prompting became too strong to ignore. As we pulled into a neighborhood to tract one afternoon, the troubled feeling was so strong that I could not get out of the car. I didn't know what to do. If we followed the prompting and did not tract at all, I worried what the district leader and zone leader would say. I was confident that this impression was not my own, but would anybody believe me? I bowed my head to pray. I pleaded to know what to do. I told the Lord that I felt very strongly that we were not to tract, but I was afraid not to. The answer came quickly, "Call President!" I picked up the phone and dialed the number for our mission president. I don't think I had ever phoned him directly before. He picked up and asked if everything was okay. I told him that we were fine, and then I went on to explain our dilemma. I explained the prompting that we had both received and my struggle to heed it. I told him of my prayer. He said calmly, "I feel the Spirit confirm to me that you are right Sister Ensign-Lewis. You are not to tract right now." I told him that I feared our district leader and, potentially, our zone leader would not understand this. He told me to tell them that we were not to tract and that we had discussed this with him. If they had any further questions about it, they could call him directly to discuss it. Period. I thanked him, and we hung up. I was so relieved. I was flooded with gratitude for an inspired priesthood leader that could confirm the direction of the Spirit. We now felt empowered.

My district leader never said anything unkind, but I knew that he wondered what we were doing. It was still enough to make me feel ill at ease when I interacted with him. My zone leader was completely respectful, taking us at our word without a single question.

I felt like an infant again. The numbers that had become my guide, my motivation, and my measuring stick were gone. The mission goals were clearly meant to help missionaries effectively engage in the Lord's work, just as the law of Moses was intended to point disciples to Christ. Most missionaries used these goals to keep their work balanced and directed, but I had come to view these expectations as the ultimate end of the law. Like the Pharisees, I had missed the mark and become obsessed with the numbers alone. I had forgotten the true purpose of missionary work: inviting children of God to come unto Christ. I had to learn how to be a missionary all over. However, this time, I was not alone. I had a companion that had been selected for me by the Savior of the world, and I was finally able to recognize that.

Our days started to look different. During our companionship study time each morning, we worked together to study the scriptures and to create inspired teaching outlines to share with active members of the ward. Both of us had received priesthood blessings that discussed the importance of our work with the members in that particular area. We searched for scriptures that would inspire the members to pray for missionary opportunities. We prayed at length over the members of our ward. Our companionship prayers grew longer, more fervent, and much more frequent. We spent a significant amount of time on our knees listening, waiting for His help and direction. I no longer tried to drag Sister Dawson out of the apartment. She departed willingly.

Without the goals and numbers to justify our work, we turned more consistently to the Lord and relied more fully on the Spirit for specific guidance throughout the day. We learned to trust the promptings we received. These promptings were our only source of direction; they became our lifeline. I found myself repenting more often as I sought so desperately for the Holy Ghost to be our constant companion. Throughout the day we would pause to pray for help. "Who would Thou have us visit? Where would Thou have us go?" We would look up at each other to communicate about the impressions we received. "I feel like we need to see Sister Hurler and Sister Parks," Sister Dawson told me after we had prayed together one afternoon. I agreed. "Sister Hurler has been on my mind all morning too. And I just felt like we should see Sister Parks while we were praying." Then we would head directly to their homes. During our service projects, the nice lady that always gave us tasks to do approached us with some questions about the Church. Dinner was not just a break anymore. It became the subject of prayer and study as we took these important moments to urge the members to share the gospel. We came home to our apartment each evening excited about the opportunities we had been given and the promptings we had received.

Nightly accountability lost its sting for me. The conversation remained, but the fear it had inspired in my soul was gone.

"How was your day, sisters?"

"It was good, Elder Clark. How was yours?" I inquired.

"It was excellent. The James family is coming to church tomorrow!"

MY MISSION HEART TRANSPLANT

"How exciting! That's great news, Elder Clark." I said sincerely.

"So what did you two do today?"

"We visited Sister Hurler, Sister Parks, and the Robinson family. Sister Hurler expressed a desire to come back to church, and we invited her to meet with the bishop. Sister Parks told us about the things that were keeping her from being active at church, and we shared a message and prayed with her and for her. We also shared a spiritual message with the Robinson family that we had prepared together in our morning study. We did some service and had a great gospel conversation with Amelia there, and we visited the Brown and Johnson families to do member work with them this evening."

"Is that all?"

"I think so." My heart was calm.

"All right, well have a good night. Keep working hard and make sure you are not slacking on strict obedience. Okay?"

"We will do our best, Elder Clark." I promised. I could tell he was unsure about what exactly to ask us, but he was doing his best to be a faithful district leader.

"Good night, Sisters."

"Good night."

After a month passed, I was transferred to a different area of the mission with a new companion. Once again, I tracted on a daily basis. The numbers that had once overwhelmed me now gently guided our labors. We tried to heed the voice of the Spirit as we worked to meet our weekly mission goals.

Even though I was a normal missionary again after leaving Manhattan, Kansas, I kept one tradition with me from that time, and it stayed with me no matter where I was. Each evening as I knelt to pray, I could picture myself having nightly accountability with the Savior. I would tell Him, at length, about some of His children. I would express my sorrows for them, my concerns, and my great hopes for their future. I would ask Him to bless them with the righteous desires of their hearts and to bless them with the strength to overcome their temptations. Tears would grace my pillow. I would tell Him how sorry I was that I was not a better instrument. I would ask for His forgiveness for my prideful actions and beg for His help to change my own selfish desires. I would thank Him for the gift of His Spirit, for all of the guidance and direction He had given us that day. I would thank Him for the scriptures and for the insights we had received during our morning study that we had shared with His children throughout that day. I would thank Him for my companions, who had changed me forever. And then I would ask, with all the energy of my heart, for His pure love.

When I left my home and family to enter the mission field, I had pictured myself as one of the ninety and nine that had never strayed far from the Master's fold. Although I believed deeply in the reality of the Atonement, I desperately hoped not to need it personally. I lived off of the praise of others and sought constantly for their approval, even in my labors as a missionary. One day at a time, one companion at a time, my eyes began to open. I came to recognize that there is no such thing as a soul that needs no repentance. The soul the Savior was trying so hard to salvage was my own. As my focus shifted toward Him, I found that I was the lost sheep in need of being carried by the Redeemer back to His fold. The greatest conversion I witnessed as a missionary was not in the life of an investigator; it was the change He wrought in my own heart.

JEANNE ENSIGN LARSON grew up in California and graduated from Stanford University with a bachelor's degree in psychology before serving a full-time mission. Shortly after returning home, she married Seth Larson and moved to Arizona where she earned a master's degree in social work from  Arizona State University. She currently lives in Prescott, Arizona, where she enjoys raising her four small children.

Was That Inspiration
or Indigestion?

Karisa McAllister

I rubbed my hands together, did a few neck cracks, took a deep breath, and wheeled my bike out the door. My trainer stifled a chuckle. Most morning exits from our missionary apartment didn't create such apprehension, but this morning was special. My trainer, Sister Perkins, wanted to try an experiment, so she announced a holiday of sorts: a day when *I* was in charge. It would be my first attempt as a missionary calling the shots. I was accustomed to following Sister Perkins around and letting her lead, but this warm November day in sunny Scottsdale would be *my* day. And I didn't want to disappoint.

We carefully maneuvered our bicycles up the apartment steps, strapped on our helmets and Book of Mormon-laden backpacks, clothespinned together the front and back of our skirts (to prevent flashing all passersby), and kicked off on our bikes. Sister Perkins had chosen her librarian outfit that morning and I was wearing my *Sound of Music* dress. We felt really cool as we pedaled past our neighbors, two guys about our age who were climbing into their yellow Corvette. We waved at each other politely.

My trainer followed close behind me on her bike (first time!) and I began looking for a street to tract. Oak Street? Nah. Palm Lane? Just tracted it. Granada Road? Ummm . . . I guess no again. I cut through the bike path at the Coronado Golf Course and decided to head down a different main road. These residential streets were all starting to look the same, and I rode past all of them, waiting for a sign or some kind of positive vibe.

"Just pick a street!" my companion shouted.

I yelled back, "I'm waiting for the right one!" We continued to pedal. Five more minutes passed and we were quickly approaching the edge of our area when all of a sudden I saw The Street. It was practically glowing.

"This is it!" I shouted, and I steered to the right, toward a lamppost where we could lock our bikes. As we pulled onto that side street, I suddenly felt a jolt. Almost at that same instant, Sister Perkins, who was following close behind, gasped. We hit the brakes, dismounted, and surveyed the situation. Our bike tires had all just gone simultaneously flat. One second all four tires were full of air, and the next second they were on the rims. It didn't take us long to discover the culprit: a pile of thorns strewn on the side of the road where we had just passed.

I just stood there with my hand over my mouth, speechless. "Of all the streets you could have picked," Sister Perkins muttered under her breath, "you chose the one with the thorn patch." I pretended I didn't hear that. I felt as deflated as the bikes. Why would the Spirit direct me here, of all places, just to puncture our tires? Had I gotten it wrong? Now what?

We abandoned my glowing street, not having knocked on a single door, and started wheeling our bikes toward the nearest bike shop, which was nearly a mile away. The store was located in an upscale shopping district, (which we never visited, due to our meager missionary budgets), and as we walked we estimated the cost of purchasing new tires. This was going to hurt. We'd probably have to sacrifice a whole month's worth of cold cereal just to cover the expense.

In the parking lot leading toward the bike store, just past the yoga studio and trendy cafe, we passed a middle-aged man who seemed to be waiting for a ride and staring into the distance as he sat on a bench. "Good morning," we greeted and kept walking. After all, we had some bikes to fix. Two minutes later, Sister Perkins froze, turned her Schwinn one hundred eighty degrees, and beelined back toward the man. Baffled, I followed her. We introduced ourselves to the bench guy (Tom), gave him a Book of Mormon, and ended up teaching him a discussion. He seemed *fascinated* with what we were teaching, a confusing change from the general attitude in our Scottsdale area. As we spoke with Tom, we learned that his life had turned upside down during those past few months. His healthy wife had suddenly died of a ruptured brain aneurysm, and his dad had passed away just nine days later. Tom felt desperate for answers and to come closer to God. He even admitted that he had recently begun struggling with thoughts of ending his life. Tom had urgently prayed for help the night before, and he suggested that maybe God had sent *us* as an answer to his prayers. We were stunned and humbled.

After we finished our conversation, wrote down Tom's contact information, and parted ways with him, Sister Perkins and I resumed wheeling our bikes toward the repair shop. It took us longer than expected though. We kept running into people who were willing to take a Book of Mormon and hear our brief messages. (This really *was* bizarre for our area.) Three religious conversations later, we finally opened the door of the bike shop. The bicycle repairman patched up our tires for a tiny fee, and as we rode back to our apartment for lunch, our backpacks were significantly emptier than when we had left a few hours earlier.

As I thought about that punctured bike tire prompting, I realized that the Lord works in mysterious ways. He had a specific errand for us that morning, and he had to get creative in order to direct our path. Sister Perkins and I would have never visited the shopping district that morning—it wasn't a P-day, we couldn't afford to shop, and we had no need to be there. Something needed to get us there so that we could find Tom (and the other three people too). In retrospect, my original impression to pull onto the thorn-covered street was probably correct. When the tires deflated, I thought I had misinterpreted the prompting, but as the morning passed I could see the Lord's hand guiding our path.

A mission gives numberless opportunities to learn how the Spirit works. Just like pitching a softball, learning a piano piece, or decorating a cake (three of my hobbies), it takes struggling and practice to get better. I like to relate personal revelation to getting a phone call from a parent. When your dad calls, he doesn't have to announce who he is—you've heard his voice so many times that you recognize it right away. It's the same way with the Spirit of the Lord: the more you've "heard" that voice, the better you can recognize it and respond to it. Understanding promptings is not easy, but a lot of repetition and practice can help.

Since the Spirit speaks in different ways and contexts to different people, it can help to see more than one perspective. I asked eight sister missionaries to help me round out the picture. Promptings were clear in some of the stories, but in others, they were recognized only later (and in one case, more than a year later). In a few stories, the whisperings of the Spirit led to baptisms, and other times they led to something less visible, but still very meaningful.

Tara Haglund

My companion and I started to fast weekly to be led to someone who could be an elders quorum president for the small, fledgling branch where we were serving. We were truly becoming fishers of men, we joked. We had trained the few women who knew how to read and taught them how to give lessons and run organizations, even though we didn't know much about running

Primary, Young Women's, or Relief Society. At least we'd seen our moms do it. The elders didn't have anyone to train, and our branch needed priesthood holders.

While fasting one sweaty day, we tracted in a wealthy neighborhood. As usual, several people told us to never bother them again, but as I walked by the house with the tall, yellow privacy gate, I glanced through a crack between the hinges. I saw some toes up on a ledge. A warm feeling immediately spread through me that *this* was the Lord's answer to our fast. I second-guessed myself. Toes? Our answer? The feeling came again, stronger. Well, I decided, God certainly knows the toes of his elect. I stopped my companion, who kept her feet turned to make a quick getaway once the yelling and kitchen-utensil-waving began. I took a deep breath, clapped my hands loudly, and yelled, "*Oí de casa,*" Hello to the house. The toes on the ledge disappeared and then reappeared under the gate with the welcome clanging of the lock being opened. The cooking noises from the kitchen continued, but no one stormed out brandishing ladles. Alexandre welcomed us in, led us to the porch, rested his feet on the ledge, and lit a cigarette. He was intrigued by our message; as it turned out, he'd been searching fruitlessly for religious truth for years.

By the second lesson, he had found it and proclaimed the Book of Mormon as his new source of truth, to be read in conjunction with the Bible! In short order, he'd also gained testimonies of *Gospel Principles*, Joseph Smith Translation, *Our Heritage*, and the Doctrine and Covenants. When he finally accepted baptism after attending our little branch for a couple of months, we wondered if he noticed that he was the first college graduate to be baptized in this city.

I returned with my family to this remote Brazilian town last year. I'd lost contact with Alexandre but was anxious to find out if he still attended church. My kids watched in shock at my un-American house approach: I clapped outside his gate and shouted "*Oí de casa!*" When he came to the door, we both started to weep with happiness. In the twelve years since his baptism, he'd been gospel doctrine teacher the entire time, and he'd also been the elders quorum president three times—with a year here or there to rest from double callings. He testified that the only way he could handle the responsibility was with the additional spiritual strength he'd found in the temple. I was so happy to see that he was still my "brother in the Lord" (Alma 17:2).

Tara served in the Brazil Maceio Mission from 1999 to 2001.

Catherine Shapiro

About halfway through my mission, it was almost transfer time. My companion and I didn't think either of us would be transferred, so we didn't worry, but I was concerned about our teaching pool. I struggled to know what direction we should take and where we could find more people to teach. My district leader had given me a beautiful blessing a few days before that inspired me to get on my knees and pray more fervently than I had before. He said there were people waiting to hear the message that I would bring them, and that I needed to seek them out earnestly, to "hunt for them under the rocks." He continued, "Pray to your Heavenly Father. Go to Him in prayer with your questions and as you do so, many ideas will come to your mind. Sort these ideas out and choose the one that will be the best for what the Lord would want."

I remember concentrating very hard and praying earnestly to know who we could teach. I sat and listened and thought for quite a while. Names started coming into my mind with a power that confirmed that they were not my own thoughts. *Lyooba, the branch president's wife. Talk to Lyooba.* Really? Why Lyooba? That was out of nowhere. I knew it wasn't from me though, so I quickly wrote down some of the thoughts I had, said a prayer of thanks, and asked for help in following through on those thoughts. The next day I found out that I was going to be transferred. Crazy! That night we went to a family home evening with our branch, and I thought it would be a great opportunity to talk to Lyooba. I told her I was being transferred in a few days to Kharkov, Ukraine. A big, wide smile spread across her face and she told me that she had a family member there who she wanted me to find and teach. Later that night, she called and gave me all of the details.

This experience confirmed to me just how much the Lord is involved in the details of rolling forth His kingdom. He knows which of His children are ready—if we are listening, the Holy Ghost will guide us to them!

Catherine served in the Ukraine Donetsk Mission from 2000 to 2001.

Janine Doot

My companion and I were placed in a new area with zero investigators and a deeply divided ward. For three weeks we walked the streets, knocked doors, and visited active and less-active members, but we saw no improvement. Frustrated with the situation, we began to throw blame on each other, which quickly drove a wedge between us as companions.

After a really long day, I distinctly remember walking fifteen feet in front of her, muttering mean things under my breath the entire way home. She was angry with me too but decided I needed my space so she let me walk in front of her. When we got home, she walked straight into the bathroom and began sobbing quietly. I heard her choking back her tears as I rubbed my tired, swollen feet. In that moment, I heard these words enter my mind, "You hurt one of my daughters. Make it right."

I felt the Spirit take my hardened heart and smooth it out ever so gently. The anger dissipated. Sadness filled its space. I knocked on the bathroom door and asked my companion for forgiveness. The Spirit taught me many things on my mission, but mostly, it taught me how to feel the presence of God and feel the love He has for His children.

Janine served in the Argentina Buenos Aires North Mission from 2005 to 2006.

Jenna Mangelson

We were off to teach Lucas, a young man in his twenties, who recently found out that his dad was diagnosed with cancer. My companion and I had a specific plan of who was going to teach what. We were both new to the mission field and felt the most comfortable splitting up the discussion our set way, so that each of us taught the same principles every time. As we began to teach though, a different way to start the lesson came to my mind. I was nervous. I didn't want to look unintelligent or frazzled, and I certainly didn't want to make my companion uncomfortable. I found myself in a battle between fear and faith. I was being prompted to take a step into the unknown, trusting that God would be there.

I took the step of faith and began the lesson in a completely different way than was planned. The Spirit filled the room. I knew my companion felt it and I knew that Lucas felt it. Because we followed those thoughts that came into our minds, we were blessed with an abundance of confidence and the influence of the Holy Ghost. The lesson was specifically tailored to Lucas, a young man searching for peace in a time of sorrow. He needed to hear the gospel message taught in a specific way. God knew which way he needed to hear it.

Jenna served in the Argentina Cordoba Mission from 2006 to 2007.

Amy Benson

I served in the French Riviera. My last area was a little port town called Antibes, nestled between Cannes and Nice on the Mediterranean coast. It was postcard-beautiful, with centuries-old buildings and splashes of flowers spilling over balconies against a backdrop of sailboats and sea. My companion and I usually had some success talking to people in the town center, a large open area with cobblestone streets and lots of little shops and people bustling about. When I say success, I don't mean teaching people discussions; I mean being able to stop people for a few seconds before they hurriedly walked away. The only thing the French people liked less than being stopped by a stranger was being stopped by a stranger who wanted to talk about religion.

One day I approached a woman passing by who looked to be in her sixties. I started with the usual introduction and that I was sharing a message about Christ when I stopped and interrupted myself. "Have you had someone close to you die recently?" I had no idea why I asked such a question—I certainly never had before. But I felt very strongly that that was exactly the thing to ask. Her eyes widened in surprise. "How did you know?" She queried. "My husband died a week ago."

I opened the Book of Mormon to Alma explaining the Resurrection and asked her to read the highlighted verses. She read them in a quavering voice, and then I promised her with certainty that her husband would be resurrected, and that one day she would see him again. I told her that God wanted her to know this. By this time tears were streaming down her cheeks. I asked if my companion and I could share more with her about this, but, to my surprise, she politely declined. She sincerely thanked me and hurried off.

The experience left me in awe. I knew without a doubt that the Holy Ghost had prompted me to ask her that question. And yet it would not result in her getting baptized. So, why? I guessed that perhaps Heavenly Father wanted to comfort a daughter of His who needed comforting. I was just blessed to be the hand that provided it.

Amy served in the France Marseille Mission from 1993 to 1994.

Jackie Shafer

My companion and I were invited in to teach an older Hispanic woman named Isabel. Isabel was very eager to talk to us. She was familiar with the Church and the Book of Mormon, but as we taught it became clear she liked our message but didn't want to leave the church she was raised in. As we began to wrap up the lesson, the Spirit suddenly filled me with power and excitement. I felt prompted to ask, "If you knew these things were true, would you follow Jesus Christ's teachings and be baptized?" My heart was pounding. I silently told the Lord, "Uh, I don't know how to say that in Spanish!" However, the prompting didn't go away.

I was desperately asking for the words to come to me, but I simply couldn't piece them together in my head.

We were about to say a prayer to end, so after a brief inner struggle, I blurted out the question as best as I could. It sounded like gibberish, and I could tell my companion knew it. However Isabel smiled and answered the question. She simply couldn't leave the church that her family was a part of, no matter what. We shared our testimonies and left.

Outside, my companion kindly asked me what on earth I meant to say. I explained it to her and she told me she didn't have a clue what I was saying. The wonderful thing was that Isabel did understand. I realized that the Lord didn't mind that I didn't know how to say it correctly—He knew if I opened my mouth, He could help Isabel understand. I was reminded once again that the Spirit is the true teacher.

Jackie served in the California San Fernando Mission from 2003 to 2004.

Chelsea Rowan

Nivia was one of the most curious investigators from my mission. She had spent some time studying with the Jehovah's Witnesses before we met her, and she had a lot of thoughtful questions about the gospel. We responded to her questions the best we could, relying on the scriptures and our testimony to punctuate our answers. Eventually, she desired with all her heart to be baptized and she joined the Church. I was very grateful that she had made this choice but wished I were better at following the Spirit's lead in a lesson. Huge, miraculous promptings never stopped me dead in my tracks during the lessons. I wondered what I was missing.

A year later, when I was teaching Spanish at the MTC, I received a letter from one of the sister missionaries I had taught a few months before. She reported that Nivia was still strong and active in the Church. Then the sister missionary asked, "How did you know which scriptures to share with Nivia? She said you flipped open the Book of Mormon and found a verse to answer every question she ever had. How was that possible? I will never know the scriptures that well."

As I read her letter, the Spirit calmly impressed my mind that I had been following His promptings all along. I wasn't a genius who somehow recognized the exact verses that Nivia needed to hear, but the Holy Ghost knew. He just passed along that information in the form of a sudden idea of a scripture verse to share and all I had to do was pay attention.

Chelsea served in the Uruguay Montevideo West Mission from 2003 to 2005.

Alyson Sawkiw

We always prayed. We always expected to be led, and we were obedient and organized. But the moments of feeling led were not the norm I expected them to be. One of my companions and I had an ongoing joke—the "let's pretend this is a missionary story that we're going to tell at our homecoming speech and repeat for years to our children and grandchildren" joke. Many days looked something like this: a feeling of inspiration to visit a certain area followed by a series of empty homes, a few girls who only wanted to talk about America, and an old man who felt it was his duty to tell us about the end of the world. Maybe there would be an opportunity to share a spiritual thought along the way. Amazing story, right? We hoped that on those days that we were striving so hard to be in the right place at the right time that someone was touched somehow. Most likely it was just us, learning about perseverance.

But then there was the day that we took the wrong bus, ended up in an area of town we didn't recognize, and decided we had time to knock on a few doors. There were no angels. I don't recall a frisson of excitement or a warm and fuzzy feeling. We just didn't want to waste the rest of the afternoon, so we decided to cross the street and knock on the first house we came to. We ended up meeting a humble family, former members of the Church who had been baptized, but hadn't been back to church since. Now married, with children, they committed to joining us the next Sunday and later became a rock in the small area branch.

The Lord told Joseph Smith, "For behold, it is not meet that I should command in all things. . . . Be anxiously engaged in a good cause, and do many things of [your] own free will, and bring to pass much righteousness" (D&C 58:26–27). This scripture was key to my mission experience. We prayed and we listened. But we also got up and got to work. The miracles, the choirs of angels, and the realization that we *had* been following the Spirit often waited for the work to be done first.

Alyson served in the South Africa Durban Mission from 1996 to 1997.

The collective wisdom of these eight missionaries is something I only wish I had before my own mission. What I noticed is that the Spirit touched people in many different ways in these stories: through warm feelings, powerful thoughts, words put into someone's head, words put into someone's mouth, a feeling of power and excitement, reminders of scriptures, and the desire to work, to name a few. The Lord's guiding hand was evident in the moment in some situations, and other times it took time to perceive the influence of the Holy Ghost. It was thrilling for me, personally, to look back and see some heavenly force working through me on the day that we rode our bikes over the thorns. This kind of guidance from the Spirit is a privilege that all missionaries can have as they live worthily and seek humbly for inspiration.

KARISA MCALLISTER was raised in Philadelphia in a family of die-hard Phillies fans. She left home to serve a mission in Arizona and attend BYU, studying speech-language pathology and music. After graduating, Karisa attended Marquette University to earn her master's degree in communication disorders. She currently lives in Milwaukee where she's surrounded by boys: her wonderful husband, John, and their three rambunctious sons.

Keep Calm and Carry Scriptures
Linda Riding Johnson

I n my worst missionary nightmare, my companion and I stood on a Scottish doorstep. "This is Sister Smudge," I said with as much enthusiasm as I could muster, "and I'm Sister Riding. We have a message for you!" The homeowner eyed me skeptically and, while shaking his head, began closing the door. "Not interested," he said as the door snapped shut. I imagined myself standing there, speechless and rejected. My concern was justified because this scene had already happened once. Shortly after my baptism, the sister missionaries took me tracting . . . on my own London street. It was a humiliating experience. The people were firm and shared the same basic message: "We are not interested." I was certain that the response from the Scots, just a few hundred miles north, would be exactly the same. What could I say that would give people a reason to listen to me?

I had listened to my high school friend, Janet, for whom talking with people was never a problem. She chatted effortlessly to everyone about everything, and when I was fourteen she started talking with me about the Church. Even though I had many religious friends, I had never met anyone who took their faith as seriously as she did. She was fifteen and a Primary teacher who regularly regaled us with stories about her class. I was particularly impressed that she took the time to read both the Bible and her sacred text, the Book of Mormon. I was even more impressed that these holy but ancient writings seemed so accessible and pertinent to my often hilarious and otherwise very trendy friend. Two years later, Janet invited me to attend a Young Women's camp somewhere in the depths of the English countryside. I met more personable and friendly LDS girls who, quite remarkably, found personal direction, inspiration, and solace in the scriptures. I was amazed that they brought their own scriptures to camp and, more important, that they referred to them often, discussing them in classes and even in private conversations with me. Their gospel knowledge led them to treat me with kindness, love, and respect. I knew that these girls loved the Lord and His word. They were noticeably different from other teenagers at my school. Although only sixteen, I could see it and feel it.

Six years later, when I joined the LDS Church, another friend kindly took me under her wing, offering to drive me to institute classes. I was thrilled to be finally embarking on a serious study of the Old Testament. I enthusiastically read and marked the first two chapters of Genesis, studied the lesson material, and attended class, all of which gave me a tremendous feeling of satisfaction. However, after one of the first classes, as I held my Bible and triple combination, I opened up the two chapters that I had read with my left hand. The weight of the rest of the scriptures lay in my right hand and, as I looked at them, I felt overwhelmed by the task that lay ahead. How could they become living bread and living water for me?

These concerns did not dampen my desire to serve a mission. While listening to the missionary discussions, I felt impressed that if I became a member, I would also go on a mission. My patriarchal blessing confirmed this feeling. This was not because I was naturally outgoing and confident. I was then a very reserved English woman and, as already mentioned, quite fearful about the prospect of standing on endless Scottish doorsteps without ever being invited into a home. Before leaving on my mission, I prayed specifically that the Lord would bless me with a loud American companion. A talkative American seemed the perfect solution for my situation. She would, I reasoned, have a great gospel knowledge, know what to say in all circumstances, and be completely fearless in talking with people (all Americans were)! The Lord heard my prayer and blessed me with a fabulous American trainer who could talk the proverbial hind leg off a donkey. I quickly learned to admire her and the way that she communicated with people. She obviously loved them, and she spoke and acted with great care and concern. I also admired the way she taught from the scriptures.

While I had obvious inadequacies, I also had faith that the Lord would help me to communicate the gospel in a loving and knowledgeable way. I realized that if I knew and loved the scriptures as my trainer did, I would have something to say to the wonderful people we met—and not just anything, but rather a personalized message from the Lord. I also realized that the word of God could have a transformative effect in the lives of those who really listened, as it had in mine.

As I read, I also discovered that the Lord had imparted wise counsel to those embarking on missions. He said, "Seek not to declare my word, but first seek to obtain my word, and then shall your tongue be loosed; then, if you desire, you shall have my Spirit and my word, yea, the power of God unto the convincing of men" (D&C 11:21). This verse provided a great pattern for me to both follow and experience as a missionary.

"First Seek to Obtain My Word":
Prayerfully Study the Scriptures

As an adult convert, I had not participated in Primary, Seminary, youth Sunday School, or Young Women classes. I entered the mission field without the benefit of formal training, as there was no MTC in Britain at the time. Furthermore, I had not read any book of scripture all the way through. How was I to obtain God's word? There were no shortcuts; it took work. The Lord says "seek learning, even by study and also by faith" (D&C 88:118). What a fabulous opportunity every missionary is given to devote two hours or more of each day to scripture study. I cherished those hours. They provided me with a spiritual education. During the course of my mission, I read all of the standard works and over thirty years later, I still look forward to my early morning scripture study. The scripture study habits I developed as a missionary continue to bless me.

Memorize Scriptures

New missionaries in the Scotland Edinburgh Mission arose at 5:30 a.m. to spend an extra hour learning the discussions and the associated scriptures before having the regular two hours of personal and companionship study. All missionaries did this until they passed off the discussions and scriptures to the assistants. In my case, it took about two months. It was a tremendously difficult but worthwhile sacrifice. Memorizing forced me to carefully consider each word in a verse. The experience was so empowering to me that I readily accepted the mission's challenge to memorize additional scripture groups. The selected scriptures were taken from basic gospel topics: the Godhead, Christ's role, the Atonement, faith, the plan of salvation, and many others. Up to that point, my experience with memorizing texts had been largely limited to a few lines of poetry in high school. I had never attempted anything like this before, and it required a consistent personal effort. I wrote the verses on cards and reviewed them during personal study time. My companion helped by quizzing me as we walked to and from our area and over dinner. Over the course of many months, I memorized about two hundred passages of scripture, but even after learning a handful, I saw immediate benefits. There is nothing quite so exhilarating or empowering as having the word of the Lord so freely available to you, popping into your mind at all sorts of times and places.

I was thrilled with the way the Lord helped me to use these memorized scriptures to teach. For example, one day we were talking with a lady who didn't like some LDS teachings. She based her objections on her belief in the Bible. However, at some later point she told us that she didn't believe in or read the Old Testament except for the books of Psalms and Proverbs. She was a Christian who confined her reading to the New Testament, which was not uncommon in Scotland. While I was surprised by how she so casually discounted a huge part of the Bible, I sympathized with her on another level because I too had been unable to understand much of the Old Testament before joining the Church and had also avoided reading it. As I thought about her comment, John 5:39, one of the scriptures I had memorized, came into my mind. We read it together, "Search the scriptures; for in them ye think ye have eternal life: and they are they which testify of me." A question I had never considered before came to me, and I asked her, "Which scriptures do you think Jesus was talking about?" Of course it had to be the Old Testament and she acknowledged that. This led to a great discussion about the value of all scriptures.

Write Talks Using the Scriptures, Spiritual Thoughts, and Impressions

In the Scottish mission, we used a study guide that helped us to explore gospel principles. (Today, all missionaries use *Preach My Gospel* for the same purpose.) Our mission president required us to write a talk each month based on a scripture theme from this study guide. His criteria were as follows: 1. Each talk needed to be carefully written out so that it was ready to be published in the *Ensign*. 2. Each missionary was asked to come to monthly zone conference ready to give the talk. 3. All missionaries were asked to mail their talks to the mission president's wife by the end of each month.

I could easily see the virtue of reading on a topic, seeking through the Spirit to more fully grasp spiritual ideas, and wrestling with how to organize my thoughts in a written format. It became an opportunity for me to express my spiritual impressions and thoughts. This process also allowed me to connect the spiritual dots. I usually began by reading all of the scriptures on a specific subject in the Topical Guide (something I had never done before), making notes on what I read, and grouping scriptures that taught similar ideas or that built on each other. As I studied, I began to see patterns and themes. I learned much by doing this. Writing up these ideas and sharing them with others added an additional layer of understanding. My topics included the Godhead, the sacrament, Christ's Church, the Restoration, the Great Apostasy, Joseph Smith, and others. Systematically arranging your thoughts and committing them to paper forces you to think through ideas more carefully.

This kind of study was also extraordinarily helpful in preparing me for different teaching situations. One evening, I was on splits with a young high-school student. We were returning to teach a family referred by our bishop. Arriving at the family's home, we noticed that they seemed uncharacteristically anxious. I asked if we could begin, but they said that they were waiting for another person to arrive. I was taken aback to discover that they had invited their local Church of Scotland minister to participate that evening to get his view on what we were teaching.

The minister arrived shortly thereafter, and, while cordial, he began lecturing us on gospel topics. He did it in such a way, without pausing or stopping or asking for any input, that it seemed impossible for us to participate in the discussion. I was amazed that a person could speak for so long without allowing anyone else the opportunity to say anything! I prayed fervently that the Lord would help me know what to do. As the minister spoke, I felt that I should try to verbalize our agreement with those things we also believed. I interjected things like, "We believe that too." The minister seemed to relax as it became clear that we held beliefs in common. He began to pause between sentences, allowing me to speak, and so I shared my thoughts more fully. I found myself saying things like, "We agree with that. There's a great scripture that goes along with this." At first I quietly quoted appropriate scriptures, but soon, as our conversation became more of a give-and-take discussion, it became possible for us to turn to and read from the scriptures together. By the end of the evening, I was even able to talk with him about doctrinal differences. I could say things like, "We see that a little differently than you," and then turn to some verses of scripture to explain some point. In my journal I noted that we talked about the Godhead, the Great Apostasy, the Restoration, the Book of Mormon, Joseph Smith, and the power of prayer—topics for which I had already written talks, in most cases. I wrote, "The only cause for disagreement was over the Church being the only true Church!" Through the Spirit and the scriptures, the whole tenor of the evening had changed and we emerged from that situation with a great mutual respect. As we concluded our discussion, he said to me, "I confess that I'm really impressed, and the thing that impresses me the most is that you used the Bible to talk with me." At the time I was greatly relieved. This gentleman was an experienced, college-trained minister and I was an inexperienced, recent convert with no formal training. I knew that the Lord had blessed me and was very grateful for it.

These practices of consistent and purposeful scripture study, memorizing certain verses, and prayerfully organizing my thoughts into a coherent written form, really expanded my gospel knowledge and understanding. It also gave me a great framework to communicate gospel principles and ideas to others. After my mission, I taught at the Provo MTC where the most common refrain I heard was, "I wish I had paid more attention in seminary!" On the other hand, those who had taken advantage of gospel classes and studied the standard works before their missions had a fantastic foundation on which to build.

"Then Shall Your Tongue Be Loosed" and "You Shall Have My Spirit and My Word"

These experiences clearly taught me the truth of the Lord's counsel, "treasure up in your minds continually the words of life, and it shall be given you in the very hour that portion that shall be meted unto every man" (Doctrine and Covenants 84:85). But I also learned that a missionary can literally be an instrument in the hands of the Lord in helping others with serious problems. Real hope, real purpose, and ultimately real conversion come as people understand and believe the word of God and then act on it. One day while we were out tracting, a woman invited us into her home. We became acquainted and began to teach. It quickly became apparent that this delightful woman was deeply troubled. She told us that she felt worthless and beyond hope because of something she had done years before. Gradually, she confided in us that she had committed adultery. She had tried different spiritual remedies without feeling any relief. She felt that the Lord would never forgive her, and the burden of remorse and sorrow she carried was overwhelming to her. As we talked, a scripture came into my mind and we read it together: "Thou shalt not commit adultery; and he that committeth adultery, and repenteth not, shall be cast out. But he that has committed adultery and repents with all his heart, and forsaketh it, and doeth it no more, thou shalt forgive" (D&C 42:24–25). I am not suggesting that sharing these verses immediately resolved her problem. They did not. But these verses gave her hope where before she had none. They gave her a reason to carry on and a reason to believe that she could be forgiven. She gratefully accepted our offer to return and teach her more, and she ultimately accepted the restored gospel.

As we used the scriptures to teach, the Spirit testified, blessed, and opened new vistas of understanding for us and for those we taught. The same is true today. My daughter, currently a missionary in Tahiti, recently wrote home about teaching a couple who "had read the first chapter of the Book of Mormon (finally after a loooong time of exhorting them to read!!), but hadn't really understood it." In this situation, what should missionaries do? Should they tell the couple, "Too bad, try again with another chapter"? No! All they needed was a little encouragement and personal help. The missionaries suggested they read the same chapter together and this time the sisters acted as guides for their friends. My daughter wrote, "We took the time to read the first chapter together, and Sœur F. and I asked questions about what was going on and made comments and they really understood it!" The sisters were able to explain and teach with the Spirit and this time their friends understood. Everyone felt the Spirit, which enlightened their understanding (see Alma 32:28). "There was seriously such a great Spirit there—it was peaceful but exciting at the same time because their minds were being opened to a new plane of learning and understanding. The Book of Mormon is seriously so powerful!" This was the perfect time for the missionaries to identify the Spirit and commit their friends to do more. That is where real change lies.

"The Power of God unto the Convincing of Men"

Ultimately, a missionary's responsibility and opportunity is to assist others to live a Christ-centered life and help them to enjoy their own spiritual experiences. Something that became evident to me very early in my mission was the correlation between serious study of the Book of Mormon and spiritual progression. Generally speaking, people who sincerely read and prayed about the Book of Mormon gained a testimony of the restored gospel of Jesus Christ. Those who did not sincerely read and pray did not. They were entertained but not engaged. To be meaningfully engaged, a person needed to be studying the scriptures for themselves, prayerfully seeking the Lord, and receiving their own witness from the Spirit. I remember one particularly frustrated missionary who was teaching me as I investigated the Church saying, "We can talk to you until we're blue in the face and it won't make any difference, will it?" I replied, "That's true. I know that you're great people and that you believe what you are telling me. But I want to know for myself. I want to feel the Spirit for myself. I want my own testimony!" As a missionary, I taught this same idea to people at the beginning of our first discussion by saying, "You can know for yourself, independent of me or anyone else, whether the message we share is true. God Himself will answer your sincere prayer through the power of the Spirit." It's a miracle because it works! We were most effective when we acted as a guide in someone's spiritual journey, helping them to experience this miracle. We did this by sharing scripturally based knowledge, identifying the Spirit, and helping others to learn how to study and understand the language of the Spirit for themselves. It is such a privilege to be a missionary who is called "to proclaim the everlasting gospel, by the Spirit of the living God, from people to people, and from land to land, . . . reasoning with and expounding all scriptures unto them" (D&C 68:1).

The Importance of Asking with "a Sincere Heart, with Real Intent, Having Faith in Christ"

I had seen this pattern of studying, praying, and receiving an answer so many times that I was confused by a situation that arose later in my mission. We were teaching a gentleman who had been taught previously by other missionaries. Our discussions with him were enjoyable, but our friend was not really progressing. It didn't make sense to me. After every discussion, we invited him to read and pray about different parts of the Book of Mormon. On return appointments he said that he had read but had no questions. This was so different to my own personal experience as well as my experience as a missionary that my curiosity was piqued. One day, when he said that he was nearly through reading the Book of Mormon, I really pressed him on this.

"What questions do you have for us from your reading this week?" I asked.

"I don't have any."

"Tell me about what you read this week," I enquired.

"Oh, I don't really remember the specifics," he answered.

Now I was really intrigued and tried to be a little more creative. "You've been reading the Book of Mormon for a while now. In a very general way, how would you summarize what the Book of Mormon is about?"

He demurred, but eventually told me that the Book of Mormon was about the Pilgrims leaving England, sailing to the New World, arriving at Plymouth Rock, and settling and colonizing America. Needless to say, we understood why our friend was not progressing.

On a related note, Moroni does not say that anyone who just picks up and reads the Book of Mormon will know it's true. There are certain requirements to receiving an answer aside from reading. He says, among other things, that we should ask "with a sincere heart, with real intent, having faith in Christ" (Moroni 10:4). "Real intent" does not mean a casual interest. Someone we were teaching said that she prayed about the Book of Mormon but never received an answer. I was surprised and asked for a little more information. She told me she prayed while lying in bed and after offering a few quick words "just fell asleep." I was happy that she had begun her spiritual journey but recognized the contrast in desire between this friend and the scriptural example of Lamoni's father, who was so intent on finding out whether the gospel was true that he offered to give up all that he possessed (Alma 22:15).

The universal need for real intent and a measure of faith struck me again in a recent conversation with a Danish convert named Maria. My missionary son and his companion gave her a copy of the Book of Mormon while they were tracting several years ago. She took the book, mainly to get rid of the missionaries, but ended up reading it in three days. Maria told me that while she liked the story, it meant nothing to her. Neither was she seriously praying about it. However, a year or more later, things had changed in her life and she read it again. This time she said, "I was more humble, I prayed, and I received an answer."

Whether in Denmark, Tahiti, Scotland, or anywhere else, when a person reads and prays with a sincere heart an answer will come.

We found Fred while tracting one day. He was friendly, but, after several visits, we knew he was not progressing at all. We had given him a copy of the Book of Mormon, which he told us he would never read. Patience is a great virtue for a missionary. Over a four-year period, nine sets of missionaries taught me. As the Lord was so patient with me, the least I could do was be understanding with others. We returned and committed Fred to read from the Book of Mormon.

The transformation in him was remarkable once he started to read. From that point, he was open to the Spirit and ready to learn. On our next visit, we had a fabulous discussion about the purpose of life. He came to Church and accepted the challenge to be baptized, praying himself to confirm the date that we extended to him. Of this event he later wrote, "The answer was quite a long time coming, but it came eventually, a feeling of great joy and a marvelous feeling of well-being." We were thrilled to participate in his baptism. The following month, he sent me a copy of a letter he wrote to the mission president explaining how he joined the Church. He related a personal experience he had reading the scriptures, in this case the Joseph Smith—History. This was Fred's personal answer to his sincere prayers, his own private miracle that occurred in the solitude of his own home through the Spirit as he read the scriptures. He wrote, "I had started to prepare a high tea [dinner] for myself. I picked up the booklet and started to read. The high tea was forgotten as I could not put the book down until I had read every word. It certainly inspired me as I knew in my heart that every word was true."

The Promises of Alma and Moroni

Alma the Younger, a powerful Book of Mormon missionary, recognized that "the preaching of the word," or using the scriptures, "had a great tendency to lead the people to do that which was just—yea, it had had *more powerful effect* upon the minds of the people than the sword, or *anything else*" (Alma 31:5; emphasis added). Alma knew that using the scriptures was essential for real conversion. He later compared the word of God, not faith, to a seed. Alma taught that if you plant the scriptures in your heart, you will recognize that the word of God enlarges your soul, enlightens your understanding, and becomes delicious to you (Alma 32:28). This he said, "will strengthen your faith" (Alma 32:30). God is true to His promises. Over the course of my mission, I experienced how this powerful formula applied to me, to those who faithfully worked as missionaries, and to the people of Scotland we loved so much and served with all our hearts.

This same formula worked for me with my own conversion experience. When I was a teenager, before I joined the Church, my friend Janet gave me a copy of the Book of Mormon along with some Church pamphlets. One of the pamphlets had an enlarged copy of Moroni 10:3–5. I liked these verses so much that I cut them out and pasted them into a book that I kept with pictures, sayings, and scriptures that meant a lot to me. I knew from the beginning exactly what I needed to do if I wanted to know whether the Book of Mormon was true; I needed to read and pray "with a sincere heart, with real intent having faith in Christ." As a teenager, I was not quite ready to do that. I was not ready to make a commitment, even though there was much that I liked about the

Church and especially Church members. But in my early twenties, I was ready to take Moroni's promise more seriously, which led me to baptism in the Lord's Church, where I continued to study His word and always had something to say—even in my worst missionary nightmare!

LINDA RIDING JOHNSON hails from London, England. She served in Scotland before venturing to America to live among the amiable people of Utah, New York, Maryland, and Pennsylvania. She loves sharing meals with family and friends, puzzling over genealogy, photography, gardening, Italy, and chocolate. She has degrees in history and special education. Linda and her husband, Karl, have four children: Joel, Ana, Sarah, and Susanna.

Swallowing My Pride (and Other Mission Survival Lessons)

Ainsley Thatcher

I thought I had the MTC figured out, for the most part. After several weeks in the place, I had finally gotten used to repeating Italian idioms for hours on end, eating lunch in ten minutes, and accepting the Froot Loop stains on my notes about verb endings. My gospel knowledge was expanding and my volleyball game had never been better.

My first inkling that the "Empty Sea" (MTC) wasn't just spiritual summer camp, and that critiques (sometimes painful) were a central part of missions, came during week five. It started out when a well-meaning teacher gave me a copy of President Ezra Taft Benson's 1989 general conference talk, "Beware of Pride."[13] He called me out into the hallway during class and handed it to me as discreetly as possible. I walked back into class after the exchange, waiting for the next missionary to be called out into the hallway for a little chat, but nobody was. I wondered why he only wanted to give feedback to me. To my surprise, the same thing happened later on in the week with the same exact talk, this time from another teacher of mine. What was going on? And then another teacher (whom I barely knew and who wasn't even my teacher) handed me yet another copy of the same talk, saying

---

13 Ezra Taft Benson, "Beware of Pride," *Ensign*, May 1989.

that she had overheard my teachers talking about their students' problems and thought I could use this. This time it wasn't funny. A few days later, I shouldn't have been shocked when an elder from my district very kindly pulled me aside and handed me a copy of—what else?—the same talk, which had really helped him, he claimed. Then on Sunday, after an agonizing week of soul searching, I thought I was in the clear until I sat down with my MTC branch president for a routine interview. During the course of the conversation, I saw him reach into his folder as if in slow motion, and watched him pull out the oh-so-familiar talk and place it before me. I was so flabbergasted that I couldn't speak. All told, in the course of seven days, I had been handed "Beware of Pride" five different times, by five different people. That's five times, from five different people. I don't remember exactly what may have prompted this "Pride Week," as I affectionately named it, but that is probably a clue that I may have had a problem, which was painfully obvious to others, but not to me.

It feels relevant to mention here that this was not some MTC tradition. We didn't normally hand each other unsolicited general conference talks like Secret Santa gifts, according to each person's glaring need for correction. I felt that I was simply terribly misunderstood (an evaluation that implied my level of pride in itself). Every way I turned seemed to land me squarely in front of another stapled copy of that talk. I was discouraged, to say the least. And really, really prideful, apparently.

It was tempting to allow myself to feel defensive or crushed, although I knew that neither response was helpful for my emotional well-being. If I was going to survive this mission, with all the awkward companionship inventories, peer reviews after role-playing, and interviews with my mission president, I was going to have to learn how to respond in a healthy way to criticism. As

I focused on working through my pride, I recalled something I had read in the months before I decided to submit my papers to serve a full-time mission. President Gordon B. Hinckley's book *Standing for Something* had had a profound effect on me and on my ultimate decision to serve a mission. In particular, the ninth virtue President Hinckley wrote about, "Optimism in the Face of Cynicism," gave me comfort. In that chapter, he wrote, "Growth comes with correction. Strength comes from change and repentance. Wise is the man or woman who, having committed mistakes now pointed out by others, changes his or her course."[14] In reality, my "Pride Week" was only a prelude to many more interactions on my mission where my shortcomings would become clear. But it was during this time that I decided I would take criticism from others positively, always striving (even humbly, when I could) to apply people's suggestions to becoming a better missionary.

In essence, I would look to a greater cause and choose to not be offended. I would try to keep in mind that people almost always mean well. I am certain that everyone who handed me that talk had my best interest in mind.

Certainly, President Benson's counsel helped me, and his counsel is something that I still have to remember regularly. Still, it was pairing those words with President Hinckley's ideals on being positive—on choosing to be happy—that got me through this emotionally depleting time. Did I need to be more humble? Clearly. But I also needed to work at that personal virtue in a productive way. The best thing I could do was to not get disheartened, but rather to take it in stride and actually learn something from the experience! Staying positive and choosing to not be offended saved me from a lot of unnecessary frustration. It helped me to

14 Gordon B. Hinckley, *Standing for Something: 10 Neglected Virtues That Will Heal Our Hearts and Homes* (New York: Three Rivers Press, 2000), 118.

change what needed to be changed, sustain my companionships, help investigators and members, and—most important—make myself available to the promptings of the Spirit. I learned quickly to allow myself to productively deal with feelings of inadequacy by taking small steps at self-improvement. It was one of the many healthy habits that germinated in the trials of my mission and helped me long afterward.

The great news is that you have eighteen uninterrupted months to develop these habits. It may seem counterintuitive to focus on yourself during your mission, but each aspect of your well-being will take on primary importance at one time or another, and all of them require attention and nurture so that you can serve others well. As a missionary you are working to paint a masterpiece, and each brush stroke makes a difference.

The not-so-great news is that maintaining health on your mission can be a challenge and not fully attainable at all times. You will almost certainly feel stress about the changing variables and tasks you face each day, and about the height of the bar that is set for missionaries in general. You will gain or lose weight. You and your companion will get sick from time to time. You will not be able to keep up that marathon training and your piano technique will get rusty. You will feel emotionally drained from long hours of allowing yourself to be accessible to the Spirit and vulnerable to those around you every place you go. You may feel exhausted as you push yourself to learn a foreign language or master the scriptures. You will lose sleep and you might even lose hair. There may even come a time, as it did at a time in my own experience as a missionary, when you question the very testimony that you bear to others each day.

The reason that it can be such a challenge to maintain your overall health as a full-time missionary is simply that you cannot control everything, nor should you try. As the Lord instructed the newly appointed seventy in the Gospel of Luke and counseled Oliver Cowdery in the Doctrine and Covenants, we are expected to leave our more vain personal traits, endeavors, and concerns behind when we commit to serve the Lord full-time (Luke 10 and Doctrine and Covenants 23: 1–2). But this does not mean that we should toss our efforts at well-being out the window. Instead, try to focus on the small things that can make a great difference in your overall success as a missionary: learning your personal limitations and strengths, getting regular physical exercise, praying diligently and honestly, using your preparation day time in appropriate diversions, practicing patience and kindness to those around you (which almost always elicits an in-kind response), getting proper rest, and finding opportunities to count your blessings, because angels will attend. Let loose! Maintain your sense of humor! You'll only go through this valley once. Make it count and make it happy.

Perhaps the most important aspect of our well-being as missionaries is maintaining a good attitude and a proper perspective. President Hinckley stated, "I have learned that when good men and good women face challenges with optimism, things will always work out! Truly, things always work out! Despite how difficult circumstances may look at the moment, those who have faith and move forward with a happy spirit will find that things always work out."[15]

The decision to be happy each day, to accept criticism humbly, and to take care of your body will change the course of your mission; it will directly affect your overall health at a time when you are unable to stop and focus acutely on your well-being. And as

---

15 Gordon B. Hinckley, *Way to Be* (New York: Simon and Schuster, 2002), 84.

you gain a testimony of the principles intrinsically linked to taking care of yourself, you will find that you can apply those principles time and time again throughout your post-mission life as a student, employee, mother, wife, ward member, and in the many other roles you will certainly play.

AINSLEY THATCHER is five feet, seven inches of inherited angst. She earned her bachelor's degree in English from Arizona State University. She spends her days trying to outfox Boston drivers, tutoring, supporting her husband during his medical residency, and raising two young children. Every surface in her home is covered in ketchup. Please send help.

Secrets of Sisters Who Did the Impossible
Elise Babbel Hahl

I am convinced that all missionaries eventually come to an area where "there's nobody to teach" and "the members just don't care," whether it's in California or the Congo. In those places, it can be hard to feel that your efforts are bearing any fruit. The natural thing to do is just to put your head down and push—push through the area and the frustration and hope for a better area the next transfer.

But two sisters, whose stories I will discuss below, did a lot more than survive in these tough places. They turned wards around, watching miracles happen in places where miracles never happened. Instead of just pushing through, these sisters redefined what was possible—truly living Paul's missionary motto: "I can do *all things* through Christ which strengtheneth me" (Philippians 4:13; emphasis added).

These sisters turned in their name tags several decades ago, but their service was remembered long after they left their missions. One of them inspired a Harvard Business School professor to write a case study about her work, and the other served so effectively that a General Authority interviewed her, trying to see whether her approach to missionary work could be taught to other missionaries too. These sisters defied expectations. In areas where baptisms were historically low, they helped to guide many people toward baptism. In wards where the members never helped, they found ways to unite the entire ward behind their efforts. They had confidence in their promptings and weren't afraid to try new things to keep the work alive.

I interviewed each of these sisters to capture what could be learned. I read journal entries and the famous case study by Clayton Christensen and asked lots of questions. One thing I noticed when I talked to them was their modesty. "You don't need to use my name," one of them said, "or maybe you could refer to me as 'Sister Blondie,' what the locals used to call me." The other woman told me, "I don't really deserve all this fame and glory. I just studied and prayed and followed the Spirit." I had to reassure both of them that I wouldn't glorify them as individuals. Still, I didn't let them off the hook. Their stories show that missionary service can lead to amazing results, and they also teach real lessons—things that we can do too.

★ ★ ★ ★ ★

Susan Fulcher[16] had been a member for only a year and a half when she was called to serve her mission in New England, which at the time was "one of the lowest baptizing missions on earth," she said. Within this lowest-baptizing mission, she was sent to one of the lowest baptizing areas—Cambridge, Massachusetts, and its suburb, Belmont. It was an area with a lot of professors and doctors, and getting into anyone's house was difficult. The members were terrific people, but since they didn't seem to need the

16 Details about Sister Fulcher's story come from a case study (Clayton Christensen, "Sister Susan Fulcher Case Study." MissionaryLeaders.org, 1999 [ed. 2010]. URL: http://missionaryleaders.org/node/41, accessed September 29, 2013.) and from a personal interview with the author. Unless otherwise noted, direct quotes come from the personal interview.

missionaries the way that other wards did, they knew less about their efforts. The missionaries complained that meals seemed to be their only chance to interact with the members, who were busy with outside obligations. As a result, the Cambridge First Ward left a lot of elders and sisters feeling frustrated.

Susan Fulcher arrived in Cambridge in June of 1978 with a different perspective than most. She was absolutely thrilled to share the gospel with others, since she knew how it had blessed her life. "I love being in New England," she would say in her light Southern drawl. "I feel like a really rich person who spends all day every day walking down the street trying to give each person she meets a one hundred dollar bill. It's funny, but I don't even feel discouraged when I ask someone to learn about the Church, and they tell me they're not interested. . . . At some point in their lives, they might remember how they felt, and remember that it came from God through me."[17]

Not only was she happy to be a missionary in such a low-baptizing place, she was thrilled to get to know the members, even the ones who weren't used to helping the missionaries. "I was just a new member myself, and so I was just excited to get to know members and work with them and help them be able to share the gospel," she explained. When she prayed to understand how she could best move the work forward, the answer was clear. "It just resonated with me that the most important thing I could do was to get to know the members."

In order to earn the trust of the Cambridge First Ward members, Sister Fulcher knew she had to show that she cared about them. She decided that one way to do this would be to show up half an hour early to church. Because it started at eight in the morning, she and her companion would have to walk out

---

17 Clayton Christensen, "Sister Susan Fulcher Case Study," 1999 [2010].

the door no later than seven to make it. Sister Fulcher's companion thought that the plan was slightly crazy. Why couldn't they just use that time to take care of stuff at home? Sister Fulcher explained her philosophy: "I think the time before church is the most valuable time in a missionary's week. If we're there, we can greet members and help them feel the Spirit as they talk to us. It's a great time for us to get to know members." They left at seven.

On that first Sunday in the Cambridge First Ward, Sister Fulcher established a tradition not only of chatting with members before church, but also of sitting next to a family for sacrament meeting instead of sitting off with her companion on an isolated pew. When the meeting was over, she cornered the ward clerk to ask for a membership list and then convinced her companion to go to Gospel Doctrine instead of Gospel Essentials, since they didn't have any investigators with them. "I just found it was important for [the members] to feel my spirit, to know that I knew the scriptures," she said.

During the next week, she used the ward list that the clerk had given her to make a chart of all the ward members, with spaces for information about their families. She prodded the ward mission leader into setting up a "Know Your Members" contest, where he would ask the elders and sisters questions about ten random families on the ward list. If the elders and sisters answered over 60 percent of the questions correctly, the ward mission leader had to buy them ice cream. They all passed, of course!

Over the following months, she involved each auxiliary of the Church in her work. She went to a Young Women's class and instead of practicing a discussion with them, as most missionaries did at the time, she bore her testimony and asked them whether they would be willing to help to decorate the Christmas tree of an old woman who was taking the missionary lessons. The Young

Women were thrilled to help. Sister Fulcher also made inroads with the Primary workers by taking over as Primary chorister one day so that she could give the regular chorister a break. Everybody knew who she was because she was helping out everywhere.

Instead of knocking on doors only in Cambridge and Somerville, the usual neighborhoods for tracting because of their high-density residential areas, she chose to tract in Belmont because it had the highest concentration of members' homes. That way, potential investigators would always have a member nearby to help, and she could stop in on members occasionally to motivate them and show that she was working in their area. "Sometimes people think, 'What do those missionaries do?'" She wanted to make sure they knew that she was working hard.

Sister Fulcher generally liked to ask newly baptized members for referrals, partially because she was a new member herself, but in the Cambridge First Ward, there just weren't any new members to ask. After consulting with the bishop, she chose to ask families who had just moved into the ward for referrals, because they had brand new pools of people to teach, potentially. She challenged one individual, a student at Harvard Business School, to invite somebody to learn more about the Church. A few months later, this student felt prompted to invite a classmate of his to hear the missionary discussions. When the friend accepted, Sister Fulcher set up an appointment immediately and asked the student to bear his testimony about asking his friend at the next fast and testimony meeting.

The members were moved by the student's heartfelt testimony about the invitation. From then on, whenever members had missionary experiences, she invited them to tell their stories over the pulpit so that missionary work would feel more doable to their friends. "Success breeds success," she said, reflecting on the testimonies. "When you hear other people saying 'this is what we did' and what a blessing it was, it was exciting, and it did spread. It got everybody in the ward excited." Soon, many more people were sharing their missionary experiences during the fast and testimony meetings, and the Cambridge First Ward suddenly had a lot going on.

Over the course of nine months in the area, dozens of members ended up referring friends to the missionaries, and many of these friends were baptized. This happened in a ward where missionaries hardly ever taught anyone, according to the mission president. Not only did the ward members welcome many new converts, the members themselves were edified by their involvement with the missionaries, and enthusiasm replaced indifference. The ward that was once such a dispiriting place to serve had found its fire. Truly, a miracle had occurred.

★ ★ ★ ★ ★

In contrast to Susan Fulcher, Julene Babbel[18] had spent her entire life hearing miraculous missionary stories and preparing to share the gospel. Even so, she spent the flight from Hawaii to Tokyo feeling completely terrified. She had been plucked out of Language Training, the 1960s version of the MTC, one month before her time was up because her mission needed her earlier than expected. She had committed one Japanese discussion to memory by that point, but it was the kind of memorization that didn't stick the next morning. Her family and friends were fasting for her as she flew across the Pacific, praying that the Lord could help her to adjust to this sudden change in plans. It was a daunting situation for Julene, who had aspired to serve in an English-speaking

---

18 Details about Julene Babbel's story come from her mission journal and from a personal interview with the author.

mission her entire life. She worried that the challenges of language and a different culture in Japan would make it hard for her to understand people and threaten her ability to testify.

Once she arrived in Tokyo, she was placed with a Japanese trainer who spoke very little English and who didn't believe in coddling. Within days of her arrival, Julene was placed in the middle of a bustling train station in Yokohoma, Japan, there to begin her new life as a proselyting missionary, ready or not.

Her job at the station was to stand there and pass out tracts, cards with information about the Church and its meeting times. With only three conversation lines under her belt, she couldn't do anything much fancier. People poured in and out of the station by the hundreds. Julene's trainer went to work, busying herself with passing out tracts and chatting with the people. Julene hung back, intimidated by the crush of people in this unfamiliar place. "I need some help here, Lord," she prayed. "I don't know how to do this."

She watched the crowds. She walked back and forth. And then she noticed something. Out of the sea of unfamiliar faces, one young woman stood out to her, almost as if there was a light shining around her head. With some trepidation, Julene walked over to this woman and began to recite her three memorized lines. "Hello, my name is Sister Babbel. I'm a missionary for the Mormon Church. Would you like to learn more about our beliefs?" The young woman said yes.

Sister Babbel didn't know what to do. She didn't have anything more to say after that! She brought the young woman over to her companion, who was able to continue the conversation and write down the young woman's contact information. Then Sister Babbel walked away, weaving through the crowds and looking for someone else who stood out to her, like the first young woman. After a while, she eventually saw a light surrounding another person. She walked up to the individual to offer one of the pamphlets. After stumbling through her three lines, Sister Babbel was delighted to hear another "yes."

In a place teeming with people, she noticed four people with the same brightness about them over the course of an hour. She tried to contact each one. One of them, a woman in a green plaid dress, ran off to a department store across the street from the station before she could be approached. Sister Babbel prayed in her heart that the woman would return to the area, and twenty minutes later, there she was again in the station. The fear left Sister Babbel's heart as she stopped this woman to speak to her, and she was delighted to find out that this woman was interested in the Church too.

Each of the four people she talked to that day accepted an appointment to hear the missionary lessons. Back in the apartment later that night, Sister Babbel's trainer was incredulous. "We usually contact one hundred people before we get one who takes the lessons, and we teach one hundred people before we get one who's baptized." In her best English, she asked, "So how come you contacted only four and they all wanted to hear the lessons?"

Sister Babbel responded, "I just asked for help to be able to recognize who I should give a tract to."

In the end, each of the four people she contacted at the station accepted baptism and joined the Church. She recognized the moment as a tender mercy of the Lord because she was struggling with the language. Experiences throughout her mission, however, helped her realize that these moments were also more than that—they were the result of powerful spiritual gifts from the Lord.

Julene Babbel found inspiration in the miraculous mission stories she heard as a child, especially those of her father.[19] These

---

19 See Frederick Babbel, *On Wings of Faith* (Springville, UT: Cedar Fort), 1998.

stories gave her the confidence that miracles not only do happen, but *should* happen to missionaries. Instead of wondering whether she would receive some of the same spiritual gifts, she *expected* that she could access these gifts as a missionary. Her confidence in these gifts allowed her to experience the same sorts of miracles that infused her family gospel discussions.

The gift of discernment had allowed her to perceive who was ready to receive the gospel at the train station, and as she grew more confident in the language, it helped her to teach her investigators as well. At one point in her mission, she was called to serve in a ward where the missionaries had a combined total of twenty-two people in advanced stages of the missionary lessons. The World Fair in Osaka had stirred interest in the Church and generated a number of referrals all over Japan. Still, none of the investigators in her new area had acted on this interest to develop a testimony of their own or commit to baptism.

Investigators didn't usually address what was holding them back, at least not directly, thanks to the rules of cultural etiquette or simply not understanding what held them back. Once Sister Babbel arrived in the area, she prayed for guidance to understand what hurdles faced each investigator. When she met with each of these investigators, she was blessed with a clear understanding of each person's challenges. Through her spiritual gift of discernment, she could tell whether someone had a problem with the Word of Wisdom, parental permission, or something else. She then offered an inspired challenge to each investigator, complete with specific tasks, which, if they fulfilled, would help them develop a testimony and prepare them for baptism.

When the investigators followed Sister Babbel's inspired counsel, they each gained a testimony of the restored gospel. One example shows how she confidently relied on the promptings she was given. Most missionaries, after teaching about the principle of fasting, might suggest that an investigator try it out at the next Fast Sunday meeting. After all, fasting is usually a new concept and one that calls for sacrifice. While meeting with one young woman, Sister Babbel felt sure that if this young woman would only fast and pray sincerely, she would receive a testimony. Trusting in this prompting, she asked her directly to fast and pray in order to develop a testimony of her own. The woman accepted the challenge and was so moved by the spiritual experience that followed that she decided to be baptized. Years later, Sister Babbel remembered the sure feeling she received before she made the challenges, which were "tailor-made for the particular person" because of the promptings she received.

★　★　★　★　★

At first glance, the examples of these two sisters might seem extraordinary and inaccessible to the average missionary. But there's a principle here that any sister can apply. The crucial element that links these two missionaries is the trust they had in the inspiration they received. They each sought for guidance through prayer when faced with circumstances that others had deemed "challenging," and they didn't allow prevailing low expectations to cloud their promptings. While other missionaries gave up on working with the members, Sister Fulcher responded to her prompting by placing all of her efforts into working with these same members. After taking a structured approach to getting to know, understand, and love them, she saw miracles happen. While most missionaries in Japan expected high levels of rejection for each person interested in meeting with the missionaries, Sister Babbel trusted that miracles came with the missionary mantle. Her miracles show how willingly the Lord provides spiritual gifts to those who answer the call, "Seek ye earnestly after the best gifts, always remembering for what they are given" (D&C 46:8).

To be clear, although you could hardly go wrong by imitating these sisters, these stories aren't here to encourage everyone to copy these methods to the letter, whatever the situation. Every missionary brings a unique set of gifts to the work, and every area has different circumstances. After all, Ammon's initial efforts led to the conversion of an entire tribe, while his missionary brothers, who were trying to do the same thing, went to prison!

Still, we can all seek for inspiration from the Lord and respond to it in our different circumstances. These sisters trusted that the Lord would make them capable of carrying the mantle they bore, and they did not trust in the "arm of flesh." The key to becoming a missionary who can change the dynamics of her area has less to do with copying exact methods than it has to do with taking initiative in turning to Heavenly Father for guidance. He will show us the best way to help move His work forward, if we but heed His promptings, going bravely wherever the light leads us.

The Unexpected

Emily Snyder

On a dark, cold evening in early November, I sat watching the leaves drop from their trees to the ground, curled up in an old chair in the middle of my apartment in St. Petersburg, Russia. Snow had fallen, but nothing stayed. It was wet and rainy and the outside lights cast a soft glow on the changing leaves. I was the junior companion at nine months out, but at times, I felt the full weight of this companionship on my shoulders. We should have been out tracting or working that night, but my companion was struggling, and so we were home in our sweats. This had become a pattern; we were probably on day three of staying indoors instead of doing missionary work.

We had been put together on an "emergency transfer." When the assistants called me to inform me of the new assignment, they shared that Sister Stevens[20] wasn't doing well. In fact, they felt that she was one step away from calling it quits and ending her mission early. She was questioning who she was, whose she was, why she was on a mission, and what she had to offer. She was hurting and broken and lost.

Had I known what was to come in my own mission experience, I would have been more empathetic, but that night looking out the window, I felt frustrated and annoyed. In all the time I had been in Russia, I had only helped with one baptism. The

20 Names have been changed.

only other family that had gotten close to baptism changed their minds when they found out they couldn't be Mormon *and* Russian Orthodox. I was supposed to be changing the lives of the Russians. I was supposed to be helping them know the love of God. I didn't sign up for a mission to sit in my apartment night after night. I signed up to teach the Russians the gospel of Jesus Christ. I signed up to introduce *them* to His love, not someone who had lived the gospel all her life.

Looking out the window, I sat there thinking of all the Russians walking the streets. Then I thought about how desperately God, as a father, must miss these children and want them to come home. I could almost feel His ache for their hardships, for their broken hopes. That night, watching the leaves fall down, I was tired. I was tired of talking and tired of trying to reignite my companion's hope. I was tired of not helping the Russians—which I thought was the point of me being there.

As I sat there confused, a thought came powerfully, "You signed up simply to teach about me." It was a startling and humbling realization. I felt like my eyes of understanding had finally opened: It didn't matter if it was the Russians or my companion, the mission I signed up for was to simply teach God's love to anyone and everyone. The more I reflected on this, the more I understood that regardless of someone being newly baptized or a "strong member" or an "inactive" or not at all interested in religion, missionary work was simply to bring people closer to Jesus Christ, even if it was only a small step. My life changed. My attitude shifted. Success was redefined. In the weeks that followed, I began to give my companion the energy and love I had previously thought I needed to reserve for investigators. I planned evening lessons with her in mind. I studied the scriptures to help answer her questions. I listened with love and prayed to know how to best help.

But then the headaches grew worse. Since I'd been on my mission, I had been getting pretty bad headaches. Most days as I sat in my chair studying the scriptures, I would turn the pages, or underline with one hand, while the other hand was pulling my hair trying to alleviate the pressure in my head. I had gone through a Costco-sized bottle of Ibuprofen and had emailed my mom for more. When she panicked about the massive quantity of pills I had gone through in the nine months I had been out, I realized just how bad things might be. I had thought the headaches were something I just needed to plow through and endure. I didn't want to be the sick sister missionary.

Sister Stevens accompanied me to see the European doctor who was contracted by the Church.

He ran a number of tests and finally ordered an MRI. Over the next few days while we waited for the results, the pain became incapacitating. I couldn't sleep at night. I would cry in pain and confusion. I found myself praying that the Lord would just let me go home. But then I instantly felt guilty. What good missionary wants to go home? Yet I was in so much pain. My heart and my head waged a constant battle.

The test results came back. The doctors said my pituitary gland was too big, and the only plausible cause was a tumor. I was going home.

Within days I had to pack and board a plane to meet with neurologists in the States. Guilt became my new companion. Had I prayed myself home? Was I wimping out? Sister Murphy, my MTC teacher, had been sick on her mission, but she just kept working. She was determined to serve. Was I giving up? If I had more faith, would the headaches go away? But I could not even physically entertain these thoughts for long, the pain was so crippling. I knew I couldn't continue.

I felt embarrassed and ridiculous that my mission president and his wife had to take time out of their busy schedule to drive me to the airport. I hated to be the problematic sick sister that others had to work around. As I tried to apologize, the mission president's wife was confused. She said, "Sister Snyder, we have to pick up the new sister anyway!" I was stunned and confused. For some odd reason there was one sister who was flying in, alone, on the day I was flying home by myself.

The masterful orchestration of this moment wasn't wasted on me. In order for this sister to arrive now, when I so desperately needed relief, she must have submitted her papers, received a call, gone to the London MTC, and had tickets purchased to St. Petersburg all in enough time to arrive the exact day I needed to go home. I think the Lord knew that I would have assumed that I had "prayed myself home" if it weren't for this signal. *He* had worked it all out long before my headaches began. *He* had planned that my time in Russia was over.

The flight home was filled with intense and numbing pain. From Russia to Denmark, and then to Chicago, the pressure in my head made me literally wonder if I was going to die. Because I was still set apart as a missionary, I didn't watch the movies or read the magazines in the seat pocket. I sat in the back row of the plane where my seat couldn't recline, staring out the window and then watching that little map showing just how much farther we had to go. It was the longest flight of my life as I desperately prayed for anything to relieve the pain. Just as I was about to go insane, we landed.

My layover in Chicago provided momentary respite. I walked around and took deep breaths. As I headed to the gate for my final flight home, I felt paralyzed. I could not bear the thought of getting back on a plane. Could I just wait there and have my parents come get me in Chicago? Could I drive home to Utah? As the gate came into view, I became frantic.

That's when I saw the backpack with a BYU logo on it. Actually, there were dozens of them. It was the middle of November, so I thought it odd to see a group of BYU students going anywhere. I soon found out that they were students from the BYU Jerusalem Center. Apparently, the political tension in the Middle East had escalated, and BYU had decided to bring that semester of students home a month earlier than anticipated.

I walked on the plane with a very different heart than I had expected. I buckled up and turned around to just to soak in the sea of friendly faces, but I stopped at a very familiar one. I let out some shocked tears and then hysteric sobs. Emily Larsen, my dear friend, who knew my heart sometimes better than I did, sat only a few rows back.

We made eye contact; I weakly cried out her name. I vaguely remember pushing people out of the aisle while I cried, not trying anymore to hold in my fear, confusion, and anxiety. Somehow Em switched seats around so I could sit by her. She made me lay my head on her lap and she calmed me to sleep. The next thing I knew, we were home. I shed tears of gratitude that the Lord again orchestrated numerous details for my sake. Would I have survived getting home without BYU students? Probably. Would I have been okay without Emily on that plane? Yes. But it was my miracle. The Lord knew how to comfort me, proving again in such a kind, tender way that He is not just a father, but my Father. I felt wrapped in His love.

★ ★ ★ ★ ★

More hospitals, this time familiar and all in English. There were no Russian guards with rifles guarding the doors, but I still felt the same throbbing pain as before. I didn't know what to anticipate. What would my future look like? Was I going to die?

After going through another MRI with home doctors, we realized that the communication wasn't clear between the Russian doctors and the mission doctor. I didn't have a tumor. I wasn't going to die. Of course, this was good news, but it came as a blow to my already damaged spirit. The headaches persisted and I didn't know why, and now I had no legitimate medical reason validating my early return. Maybe I really was a failure. Maybe I really did pray myself home. Or maybe I just couldn't handle being a missionary.

My mom started taking me to doctor after doctor. No one could explain or help alleviate the pain. The emotional drain on my family strained our relationships. Month after month of tests and more tests with no answers, my family's life was consumed by my pain and revolving around my problems. I would cry in my bedroom listening to the turmoil I had created. I had only ever wanted to be a peacemaker. And now, I was the cause of frustrations. I was the center of so much family pain. I felt myself slipping deeper and deeper into discouragement.

And the pain of the headaches hadn't left. They were so bad that I couldn't study my scriptures because it hurt to really think. I couldn't pray with intent, because it felt like my head was going to burst. Not only did I feel I was ruining my family, but I couldn't even keep up the habits of a good returned missionary. I shouldn't have been surprised when the depression began to seep in. After so many months of pain, sorrow, and confusion, nothing made sense. I was reaching a low I hadn't known existed.

Thankfully, I started seeing a therapist.

I am not sure how it all happened, but my mom found him and decided I needed help. I was led to a room that overlooked the Salt Lake Temple. When I saw the angel Moroni from where I sat, I felt a tiny flare of hope.

When the therapist shared that he had been a mission president, I let myself trust him. I felt that he would have compassion for my missionary heart. I cried to him about failing as a missionary. I told him about how long it took for me to finally understand my role as a missionary. I told him about wasting so much energy and not helping my companion. *And* I didn't help any Russians! I cried that I couldn't pray real prayers or study my scriptures anymore—it physically hurt. I wanted to show my gratitude to the Lord, but I also wondered why all of this was happening to me. I wondered if I just wasn't doing enough. I wondered what I did wrong to make things end like this.

I caught myself sounding like Sister Stevens—confused, lost, and hopeless. I knew that those feelings were wrong, but I couldn't shake them, and the doubts filled my mind. When I had finished expressing all my fears, this good man simply stated, "You can't earn the Lord's love."

Quietly, I tried to make sense of this concept. He continued, "There's nothing you can do to change how He values you. Your worth and His love will never change."

I had finally stopped crying enough to truly hear him. The weight of this truth began to settle. Of course I had more questions.

"But then why am I supposed to read my scriptures? Why do we go on missions or go to the temple? Or go to church or pray?"

He handed me more tissues. "So you can come to know Him. Do you feel that you know Him personally, Sister Snyder?"

I thought about special sacred moments when I had communed with heaven. I thought about scripture studies on that old, worn chair in my apartment in St. Petersburg. I thought about sacred moments that led me to my mission. I remembered the many sweet moments with the Spirit while I was writing and reading. Then there were the moments in the temple when my heart felt like it would burst with peace and joy. I also recalled the kind miracles I had felt on my return trip home. The answer to his question became clear. I did know God personally and individually.

I walked out a new person, a weight lifted from my shoulders. For the first time in months, my broken heart, soul, and body began to felt peace. I wish I could say that I was instantly healed, emotionally and physically. I wasn't. It took time for the headaches to dissipate. It took time for my heart to accept that I was enough. Oddly, it took about eight months, the same time it took for my MTC companion to come home from Russia. My "mission" seemed to finish right on time.

★ ★ ★ ★ ★

It has been thirteen years since my mission.

When I turned in my papers, I had no idea what I had signed up for. I had no idea how truly broken I would become. I had no idea the depths of pain and confusion I would experience. So many people say that their years on the mission were the best years of their lives. I would never say that. But my mission gave me the greatest years *for* my life—mainly, because I have learned to be okay with broken dreams and broken expectations.

I wish I could say that I never question and that I never doubt why certain things have happened. I still shed tears over things that haven't happened the way I had expected they would. I am still waiting for many of my hopes and desires to be fulfilled, but I have learned the absolute beauty and power of broken dreams. My brokenness bonds me to my Savior and makes me more of who I ultimately want to become. Because of my mission, I cannot doubt His love and His hand in orchestrating the details of my life. It has all been worth every tear.

EMILY SNYDER is the assistant to Clayton M. Christensen at the Harvard Business School. As a former school teacher, she adores every one of the hundreds of students she has had the privilege to teach. Emily has been an assistant to the Relief Society general presidency, is a connoisseur of chocolate chip cookies, and calls beautiful New England her home.

The Miracle of Santy

Elise Cannon

Twenty years before I started my mission, Elena Moro joined the Church. She was a beautiful Spaniard, tall and slender with red curly hair, who taught English at a local school in a city called Gijon nestled on the northern coast of Spain. Her faith had grown during the discussions with the missionaries, and she knew that baptism was the right step. There was only one problem.

Santiago, her husband, wanted none of it. He tried to convince Elena to pull out of Church, reasoning that she would soon realize her new religion was a hoax. She didn't. He tried to keep her from reading scriptures. She wouldn't. He tried burning her books, and he even considered divorce. She stayed strong in her faith.

Santiago finally decided to give in and accept her membership in the Church. He and Elena worked out an understanding: he would dedicate himself to her and their three children. He would accept her membership in the Church, as long as she would never pressure him to investigate or join the Mormons.

Twenty years later, when I began serving in the area of Gijon, Spain, Elena was still faithful in the Church and consistent in her activity, even though her husband hadn't shown any interest. As a sister missionary newly assigned to Gijon, I walked up the steps to Elena and Santiago's apartment together with my companion, where Elena was home alone that afternoon. We were going to invite her to be a part of our twenty-one-day challenge, and we didn't know how she would react. In this program, initiated by our mission president, members made a list of friends and family they could potentially invite to meet with the missionaries, and then we challenged them to read specific scriptures each day as they pondered their list. We hoped that at the end of twenty-one days, someone on the list would be ready to hear the discussions or come to sacrament meeting. We just weren't sure whether Elena would be interested in nudging Santiago toward the Church, considering their history.

Elena greeted us with an upbeat smile. To our surprise, she committed to the challenge once we explained it to her. "I will start tonight and will include my family on the list," she said. Her faith impressed us.

Not long afterward, Elena called us up to tell us that a miracle had happened with her husband. She had invited him to attend a branch activity, his first one ever, and he had accepted! Elated, she told us over the phone that she knew this was a result of the challenge we had given her.

We were thrilled to see Santy (as everyone called him) at the branch activity. He stood barely an inch taller than Elena, broad shouldered with white hair, wearing the prosthetic limb that he often wore in public (after losing his right arm in a childhood accident). He and Elena enjoyed themselves, sharing inside jokes and playful banter. They seemed to love each other deeply. To our delight, at the end of the evening, he remarked to his wife, "Those Mormons aren't so weird. They're actually normal!" We were all delighted that he felt that way—never mind that he had been *married* to a Mormon for quite some time.

He became more open to receiving our visits. Santy agreed

to teach us to cook, and while we were there, we began to chat with him about the gospel. The funny thing was that when Santy shared his thoughts and beliefs with us, they aligned exactly with our beliefs. He admitted to us that he believed in God and knew he could receive answers to prayers.

I asked, "If you know you can receive answers to prayers, why haven't you asked God if The Church of Jesus Christ of Latter-day Saints is the only true church on the earth today?"

Santy, with his big dimpled grin, replied, "I have."

We were shocked. I probed, "Did you get an answer?"

Without skipping a beat, he said, "Yes it's true. I know it's true. Besides, my wife doesn't make mistakes, so that's another reason why it's true." As my companion and I walked home in awe of what had just taken place, we felt immense gratitude for Elena. She had the faith to do the twenty-one-day challenge and to be diligent in her prayers and scripture study.

We knew it was time to help Santy move forward in his study of the gospel and ultimately, take the next step of baptism, so we devised a plan. We wanted to ask him the same question that Alma had asked his people at the waters of Mormon: "What have you against being baptized in the name of the Lord . . . that he may pour out his Spirit more abundantly upon you?" (Mosiah 18:10). We walked up the stairs to Elena and Santy's apartment on the appointed day, eager to present the question to Santy, but when Elena opened the door looking sad, my heart sank. Santy was not there. He was at the local bar with his sports club watching the soccer game. Disappointed, we still shared our message with Elena. We read Mosiah 18 and told Elena we felt strongly that her husband was ready to progress toward baptism.

Elena's eyes were wide with shock. Her lip quivered as she said, "I want Santy to be baptized, but he has already made so much progress. After drinking and smoking for years, he has given up both. He has attended a Church activity. He has met with you and continues to talk with missionaries. If we challenge him now to be baptized, you will have to teach him the discussions, and that may upset him. Then he will want nothing to do with the Church or you both again." I saw hesitancy in her pleading eyes. I earnestly prayed as I listened to her concerns. We needed help convincing her that challenging Santy to be baptized was the right thing to do. God had been preparing him for this next step for years. Of this we felt confident.

Suddenly, with determination in her eyes, Elena turned to us and said, "Okay. If it is the right time to push Santy toward baptism and the Lord thinks it is time, let's all kneel down right now and each say a prayer. If he is ready, Santy will come home from watching the soccer game at the bar." We answered with a resounding, "Let's do it!"

The moment I knelt down, the realization of what we had committed to do began to weigh heavily on my mind. I was worried that we were asking for a sign, and I wasn't sure if that was appropriate. Anxiety overcame me. Questions zipped through my mind. Were my intentions pure? Was Santy really ready? Was it really a prompting to take this next step with Elena and Santy or was it just our own feelings as ambitious missionaries? Did I just want to see a baptism or was this truly guidance from God to push Santy? I didn't know the answers. I envisioned how crushed we would all be if he didn't come home. I worried that I would lose confidence in my ability to receive revelation, and, more important, I worried that Elena would lose faith. The outcome of this prayer was significant—for better or worse.

As I sought comfort amidst these distressing thoughts, wondering if we should instead just ask for the will of God to be manifested to us, a scripture came to mind: "Yea, and they did obey and observe to perform every word of command with exactness; yea, and even according to their faith it was done unto them" (Alma 57:21).

I knew that it was according to faith that miracles happened. My bosom began to burn within me. I received confirmation again from the Spirit that Santy was ready. If we wanted to see a miracle, we had to ask.

We knelt down, our knees cold and uncomfortable on the wood floor. Each of us took turns saying a prayer. The Spirit of the Lord seemed to engulf the entire room. I feared moving would disrupt it. At the end of the prayers, I looked into the eyes of Elena and Hermana Jensen, and we had a silent conversation. We felt the power of the Spirit. After a few seconds—which felt more like an eternity—Elena went into the kitchen to make some hot chocolate for us. Suddenly, we heard the doorknob turn. A frantic Elena came rushing back to the living room, nearly knocking things over as she slid across the floor. Santy's warm, loving smile greeted our own exuberant faces. Elena could hardly hide her own amazement and curiosity when she excitedly questioned Santy why he was home. He looked perplexed as he glanced at us and then back to Elena. "I don't know why I'm home," he said. "I just felt like I needed to come back." It was a miracle. My heart burst with gratitude to Heavenly Father for answering our prayers. Again, Elena locked eyes with me and my companion. Speaking English so Santy couldn't understand she said, "Look! He came home! He really came home!" The excitement between the three of us was palpable. Santy looked at us as if we were keeping a secret but didn't question our excitement. He casually walked into the living room and sat down on the couch, inviting us to join him. This was not only a witness that God wanted us to challenge Santy, but that Santy was sensitive and listening to the Spirit. He had come home.

We knew that this was not the end. My companion and I were often reminded that Santy had to feel the guidance from the Spirit in order to change and take the necessary steps to progress. If we tried to deliver the memorized discussions, Santy would respond with, "I already know that." We had to truly seek the Holy Ghost before teaching him. Only Heavenly Father knew where Santy was in his progression and what he needed to learn.

One evening as my companion and I prayed and studied, we felt impressed to call our mission president, who volunteered to write Santy a letter exhorting him to be baptized. Hermana Jensen and I wrapped up a Book of Mormon like a present with gold paper and a red bow, and tucked the seven-page letter from the mission president inside. With giddy excitement, we met with Santy and Elena. We expressed our love for this couple, who were like family to us in Spain, and then we presented Santy with our gift. With childlike enthusiasm, Santy grabbed the gift. Gingerly, with his one hand, he felt around the edges of the gift and began sniffing the gold paper. He coyly glanced in our direction and said, "It smells like, it smells like . . . a Book of Mormon! Now you've obligated me to read that!"

Giggling at his feigned surprise, I told him, "We know we can't give you a testimony, so this was the next best thing." We invited him to read it, study it, and pray to know if it was true. We told him we wanted what was best for him and testified that we knew the only way he could have a fulness of joy was through the gospel of Jesus Christ.

Santy feasted on the Book of Mormon, and we brought him lists of scriptures to read on a daily basis. He asked questions and searched for the answers. Tenderness and humility began to show in his countenance and in his interactions with others.

As we witnessed daily miracles and subtle changes in Santy, I went through a hurricane of emotions. One day my heart would soar as I thought Santy was going to get baptized; another day, I would feel dragged down to despair when he told us that he did not know or understand enough to make that decision. Weary of the emotional roller coaster, and recognizing that Santy had already overcome so many obstacles that typically keep people from joining the church, I invited him to be baptized in three weeks. Santy incredulously exclaimed, "That's way too soon. I can't. For me to get baptized in three weeks, it would take a miracle."

With determination, my companion and I said unanimously, "We believe in miracles."

There was an unshakable determination in my heart. I knew he would do it. Our job was to prepare him the best we could. If we wanted to see the miracle, we had to ask for it, so we did.

Over the following three weeks, we flooded Santy's home with member visits. They shared their conversion stories and often expressed their gratitude that missionaries had encouraged them in their progress toward Christ.

One Saturday evening, Santy haunted my thoughts. I knew I was serving in Gijon for him, that he needed to get baptized, and that transfers were coming up. I could be leaving the area. Pleading with Heavenly Father all through church that Sunday, I prayed Santy would set a date for his baptism. In the middle of church, a member of the branch presidency hurriedly entered the room. "Santy is getting baptized. He set the date for two weeks from now." Pure euphoria filled my soul!

Reminding myself that I was in a church, I walked as fast as my legs could carry me to Santy who was fighting back the tears in his eyes. Our eyes met and he whispered, "I'm scared, but I've known I've needed to do this. I'd like to do it before you leave."

Gently Elena reminded him to make sure he was doing it for himself and not for her or for me. He calmly proclaimed, "I'm not doing this for anyone but myself. I've known that I needed to do this, and it is time."

Once I reached my missionary apartment, I let my own tears flow. I just knew he would do it! We knew that the whole experience was happening because of the steady faith and love of his wife. Santy was studying the scriptures, praying, going to church, and seeking for opportunities to serve others. When people feel the love of God in their lives and come to know him better through the scriptures, they want to do what the Lord commands.

Santy glowed with excitement at his baptism. As the brother who was baptizing him lifted my dear friend out of the water, Santy and I locked eyes. His beaming smile and glistening eyes matched mine. It was all worth it; we both felt it. People gathered around, anxious to shake his hand and welcome him into the Church, but I watched Elena. As she stood by his side hugging and kissing members, I could see in her tear-streaked face an excitement and gratitude that this day had finally come. She would have her husband by her side at church and hopefully for eternity.

Santy's baptism was a miracle. It taught me that when we put our faith in God and pray to him with all the energy of our hearts and then work as if everything depends on us, miracles happen.

One year later, I walked hand in hand with Elena and Santy as we entered the Madrid Spain Temple, where they were going to be sealed for time and all eternity. Several members who had attended Santy's baptism greeted us with hugs and kisses. Some of them had even attended Elena's baptism twenty-one years before. I embraced my two companions who had helped me to teach Santy. Then Elena grabbed my arm and introduced me to the American missionary who taught her the gospel and gave her the gift of the

Holy Ghost more than twenty years earlier. He was there with his teenage daughter. I could see the excitement in his eyes.

As Santy and Elena's sealing began, I grasped hands with my previous companions, beaming, barely able to see through the tears. I thanked Heavenly Father for letting me witness this moment. Elena and Santy stared at one another with tears flowing down their faces, holding hands, and stealing a kiss or two.

That day, I knew what heaven was like. Watching Santy and Elena create a link in their family chain that would unite them forever—this was what life was all about. Together with so many people I loved in that sacred place, I realized that we were here on earth to help each other get back to Heavenly Father.

I asked the missionary who taught Elena if he ever thought this day would come. He had been there when Santy rejected everything that had to do with the Church. He shared with me something I'll never forget, "Blessings of the mission never stop." As I watched the miracle unfolding before my eyes, I already knew he was right.

A Texas native, ELISE CANNON was excited to be called to serve in Spain. A BYU graduate in recreational management and youth leadership, she has enjoyed her opportunities to work with youth at the Boy Scouts of America and Especially for Youth. Now living on the east coast where she works for Franklin Covey, she enjoys the adventures life has to offer.

Afterword

A mission can feel like forty years of experience crammed into eighteen months. During the first months in the MTC, you may feel like a four-year-old missing her mom and dad. A year later, you may complain of back pain and long to put your feet up and rest, like a middle-aged curmudgeon. It's true what they say: the days feel like years and the years feel like days. As you can imagine, such a fast growth curve makes for a pretty wild ride. An emotional roller coaster at the best of times, you find yourself basking in joy one minute and then fighting discouragement the next. Coming home is no different. You cry in your release interview when your stake president asks you to take off your name tag, but you also cry when you see your favorite pair of high-heeled shoes waiting for you in the closet.

Perhaps these messy emotions are why returning to normal life can be so problematic. Suddenly all the things you trained yourself to avoid for so many months are accessible. Normal life does not accommodate missionary life well, so maintaining all those wonderful habits you formed on a mission feels frustrating and difficult. You may feel lost and awkward and uncomfortable: a greenie in a new area, only this time, you have no trainer to see you through it. Mission problems (like planning where to tract if your appointment falls through) change to life problems (like planning what you will study, which career you will pursue, whom you will marry, if you will marry, and a whole host of other complicated realities).

As a missionary, you were like Peter stepping out of the boat, taking shaky, miraculous steps on the water to meet Jesus. Your faith focused and strong, you believed you could do anything (and often saw miracles because of it). Upon your return, you may suddenly realize how strongly the wind and waves are whipping against you and find yourself sinking.

If you do, remember that even after Peter sank, he reached out and the Lord saved him. In fact, every time Peter lost his way, he was redeemed and *strengthened*. After all his mistakes, some which caused him to weep bitterly (Luke 22:62), Peter still went on to lead the Church. Our mistakes are important. They remind us of our dependence on the Savior. Like Eve said, "Were it not for our transgression, we never should have . . . known . . . the joy of our redemption" (Moses 5:11).

Whatever storm of life may whirl around you after you return, the answer is still the same as it was during those rough seas on the mission: keep your eyes fixed on Christ and keep walking. Don't lose faith. Seek for His guidance; pray for His forgiveness; and with those beautiful, imperfect feet, run toward the mountain to keep publishing His peace (Isaiah 52:7) (even without your name tag as a security blanket). You may want to hang onto those flats, though. Running should definitely not be attempted in heels.

Acknowledgments

A project like this always takes a village to complete. We have so many people who have supported us in our greatest hours of need. Thank you especially to our husbands, Oliver and Kurt, for their enduring patience and support of this undertaking. Both men spent many sleepless nights serving as a fresh set of eyes for the essays or a fresh set of hands to deal with tired children, all so we could get this manuscript just right and submitted on time.

Thank you to Kristine Haglund, Kent Bowen, Neil Hahl, James Engebretsen, David Babbel, Fred and Jolene Rockwood, Ken and Shari Knight, Melissa Adams and the rest of the Rockwood clan for being wonderful sounding boards and incisive judges.

Thank you to Mary Jane Babbel for dropping everything to come help out.

Thank you to Mackenzie Neuenswander for your fearless babysitting, as well as Ali Budz, Amanda Couch, Eleanor Carlile, Jane Harris, Erika Sorenson, and everyone else who helped.

And finally, we thank our children for being patient as we put this book together. This book is for you!